GW00634479

My Nigerian Journey

A Narrative of my Eighteen Years Spent in Nigeria

Myra Meehan

The Pentland Press Limited
Edinburgh · Cambridge · Durham

© Myra Meehan 1993

First published in 1993 by
The Pentland Press Ltd.
1 Hutton Close
South Church
Bishop Auckland
Durham

All rights reserved.
Unauthorised duplication
contravenes existing laws.

ISBN 1 85821 089 5

Typeset by Elite Typesetting Techniques, Southampton.
Printed and bound by Antony Rowe Ltd., Chippenham.

For
Tony

Contents

Foreword

Although I had written short articles for magazines and periodicals I had never really thought seriously about writing a book. However, after my husband Tony's book *Goodbye Maigida* was published, several people asked me to write up my own experiences of my life in Nigeria. During my sojourn in that country I had kept very comprehensive diaries of our day to day activities and on reading them I realized that in many ways my life out there had been unique.

While I was in the country I saw many changes on the political scene. When I arrived in 1951 Northern Nigeria was a British Protectorate. In 1959 self government was granted to the Northern Region and in 1960 was given to the whole of Nigeria.

Later I was to live through more troubled times, the tribal massacres in Plateau Province, civil war, assassinations and a military coup. With one exception I have not mentioned any of these events. This is essentially a personal story and volumes have been written about the political changes by people who were experts in their field, and much more knowledgeable on these subjects than I was.

The one exception I have made was regarding the tribal massacre in Plateau Province. As these massacres touched us personally I have included a brief account in this story.

I have titled the book *My Nigerian Journey* because essentially that is what it was. The first part was an actual journey done largely on the flat of my feet through the Bauchi, Gombe and Wase Emirates. These experiences were practically unique because, in my reading of the lives of women missionaries, government officials and explorers, I never found any women who lived for such long periods in such makeshift conditions with the possible exception of Ola Williams, the wife of another geologist working for A.T.M.N. who on an earlier bush tour had trekked in the Northern Cameroons.

The second part of the story was mainly a journey in time, and my day to day experiences were similar to those of many women whose husbands worked in government or private positions as well as women missionaries in the various religious denominations and female government officials.

Although many of the people mentioned in the book are now dead I trust that my stories have not caused any offence as my diaries were written 'with malice towards none'.

One difficulty I have encountered in writing the book is that since I wrote my diaries the name of practically every African country has been changed. To get over this bother I have generally quoted both names. Regarding the names of the various villages that we passed through while on trek many do not appear on any map. They were in remote areas which had never been mapped.

Regarding the information on the tribal markings of the Pagan tribes I am indebted to the official reports of O. Temple, published by C.M.S. Bookshops, Lagos.

I also acknowledge the story of the leopard episode in Jos as taken from the *Nigerian Citizen* dated April 10th 1952.

As the book is really complementary to that of my husband Tony, *Goodbye Maigida*, and as we shared most of the experiences over nearly twenty years I have tried to keep any duplication to a minimum. One or two stories appear in both books but as they were written from a different angle there is very little repetition.

Last and not least, my thanks to husband Tony who checked the details on the mining and geological aspects of the story as well as typing the manuscript.

Chapter 1

Leaving Australia

Difficulties in getting information about Nigeria . . . The journey to Capetown . . . The voyage to Lagos . . . From Lagos to the Plateau.

Only once in my life have I had my fortune told. It was in Melbourne Australia. Looking back I suppose it was the usual prophecy that would be given to any young girl. A lady, suitably attired in a gypsy costume, gazed into a crystal ball and told me among other things that I would marry and have two children. Then peering more intently into the crystal she said, 'I see you living in very strange ways in very strange places.' Well, I did marry, I did not have the two children, but regarding the last part of the prophecy I don't think either the fortune teller or I had any idea just how strange the ways or places were to be.

My first experiences came when as a young girl I lived in remote areas of rural Victoria and later, after my marriage, I went to live in outback Australia, but even these had not quite prepared me for living in isolated parts of Nigeria in West Africa.

When the time came for us to leave Australia we were faced with the choice of Peru or Nigeria. My husband had been offered positions with companies in both these countries and after considerable discussion, the toss of an Australian two shilling coin decided in favour of Nigeria. It was fortunate for us as many years later a university professor from England visited us when we were living near Jos. As a young man he had worked in Peru as an exploration geologist for the mining company which had offered Tony the position. He said conditions of living were harsh as the mine was situated at an elevation of more than twelve thousand feet which made everyday living very difficult and very uncomfortable.

1

Tony had to leave for Nigeria almost immediately. He was to work as an exploration geologist for the Anglo Oriental Nigeria Company. This company was also known as the Amalgamated Tin Mines of Nigeria or, more commonly, as A.T.M.N.

The mine or actually collection of amalgamated mines was situated on the Jos Plateau of Northern Nigeria and extended over a large area of the plateau. The mining was almost entirely alluvial mining, but the company also held leases in other parts of Nigeria, and these areas were to be prospected for lead and zinc. It was for this reason that Tony was employed as he had worked on lead-zinc for Mt. Isa Mines. Part of the contract stated that I could not join him until he had completed eighteen months of his three year contract.

During these eighteen months I tried to find out as much as possible about Nigeria. This was not easy. Very few of our friends had ever heard of the country, but one or two had known people who had gone as missionaries to West Africa. They usually concluded their remarks with, 'They died out there.' Nigeria's reputation as 'the white man's grave' was certainly well founded in the days of the early explorers and settlers, as cerebral malaria, yellow fever, blackwater fever, plus lesser known tropical diseases like leprosy and sleeping sickness took a very heavy toll.

However, after the Second World War better medicines and treatment had been found for malaria, and blackwater fever while, thanks to inoculation, yellow fever was no longer a problem.

I tried to buy a map of the country, but this proved to be a futile exercise. People volunteered information on Rhodesia, Algeria, South Africa and Egypt. In the end I decided that most did not know the relative positions of Cape Town and Cairo and the only way I could find out about West Africa was from someone who had lived there. I did hold one trump card for, living on Lord Howe Island – a beautiful island in the South Pacific which I often visited – was an old friend who as a young man had lived in Ashanti. As I wished to say farewell to friends out there I decided to go out and consult Mr Bushell.

He kept me entertained for hours telling me about life in West Africa, and although I thought some of his tales about spitting cobras etc. were a bit far-fetched or perhaps alcohol induced I subsequently found that his stories were basically true, although it was not until some years later that I learned that of the six young men who had gone to Ashanti only two were alive at the end of eighteen months. Mr Bushell had kindly kept this fact from me. He must have been a tough character as he lived to be nearly ninety-one years old.

I had hoped that when Tony reached Nigeria I would receive more information regarding the country, but letters were rather infrequent, and seemed to be mainly about bush experiences, and very little about domestic matters. My sister, a rather pragmatic type, said, 'He must be getting cornflakes or we would have had a cable.'

I was living in a medical household at the time and Doctor was worried at some of the photos Tony had sent. He had gone much thinner and appeared to be suffering from tropical ulcers. Dr Browne had been in New Guinea during the war years and was familiar with tropical diseases. He kindly provided me with some basic medicines to take with me to Nigeria.

I was able to leave Australia a little earlier than anticipated. The war in Korea was not going at all well and I told the company manager in Sydney that if I did not get away sooner than the eighteen months stipulated in the contract I might not get away at all. I then received a cable, 'Come to Nigeria at once'! There was now a frantic rush to get things ready. The Sydney office arranged a sea passage for me. The route was via South Africa, and I was to trans-ship in Cape Town to a small ship sailing to Lagos via Takoradi and Accra on the Gold Coast, now Ghana.

The next concern was regarding the health regulations. Inoculations against smallpox and cholera were obligatory and typhoid and anti-tetanus were also on the list. The only typhoid injection I could get from our local medical practitioner was something which had been prescribed for soldiers during the war years. It must have been excessively powerful, as for three weeks after the injection I could not lift my left arm. There was still the problem of inoculation against yellow fever. This was not done in Australia at the time so I was told by the authorities that I would have to get it done in Cape Town as I would not be permitted to enter Nigeria without it. Eventually all the health regulations were sorted out and then the trouble began with my passport.

At this time there was a regulation in Australia that a wife had to have her husband's permission to leave the country. When Tony left neither of us had given a thought to this regulation. The authorities now demanded that I had to produce this evidence before my passport could be issued. I pointed out that I had no hope of getting the permission before the ship sailed as my husband was somewhere in the wilds of Africa and communication was almost impossible. Finally I convinced them that I was planning to join my husband and not leave him, so forty-eight hours before the ship was ready to sail I received my passport. In the midst of all the bother over the issue of the passport my tickets for my departure arrived from our Sydney office. I was somewhat amazed to find that instead of the expected ship ticket to Nigeria I had received airline tickets for myself and daughter to Singapore. I dare say I was no more surprised than a lady in Sydney who had received ship's tickets from Melbourne to Cape Town and from Cape Town to Lagos. The office in Sydney looked after the staff supplied from Australia for the two companies, the Anglo-Oriental Malaya, and the Anglo-Oriental-Nigeria; hence the mix-up with the tickets.

Eventually everything was sorted out except the matter of what was really necessary in the way of clothing. I knew that I would need good comfortable shoes as I had been told that I would be doing a lot of walking. There were still in Australian cities army disposal stores selling ex-army surplus goods so I visited one in Melbourne which had surplus goods from the New Guinea campaign, I bought two pairs of khaki jungle pants and a white pith helmet. A relative who was with me on this shopping spree nearly passed out at the sight of me on a near freezing day in Melbourne wearing a fur coat, and then topping it off with a white pith helmet. The pith helmet was carefully packed for me and I hoped that I would never have to wear it, but as events turned out I wore very little else except the jungle pants, a couple of cotton blouses and my pith helmet during my two bush tours in Nigeria. Nearly all the remainder of my wardrobe had eventually to be left with a friend in the mining company.

At last everything was ready. The ship on which I sailed was the *Corinthic*, a beautiful cargo-passenger ship of the Shaw-Savill Line. She carried about seventy passengers, many of whom were travelling to Cape Town, and then trans-shipping to vessels bound for various African countries.

I had asked my parents not to come to see the ship sail as I knew that my departure would upset them very much, but my friends gave me a wonderful farewell. I think most of them were convinced that they would never see me again and they were more than generous with farewell gifts. Apart from the magnificent flowers there were chocolates, cakes, and enough medicines and cosmetics to stock a small chemist shop. As a bit of a joke my cousin had put in a tin of Insectibane. This was a very reliable, and practically all-purpose insect repellent, guaranteed to kill fleas, ants, bugs etc. and was much used in Australia at that time. I packed it away in the corner of a suitcase and promptly forgot about it. It was to prove very useful later in the journey. As food was still rationed in England I gave the fruit cakes to friends on the ship as, apart from not really requiring them, I did not think that they would travel very well in the humid tropical atmosphere of West Africa.

When the steward came to the door and saw the cabin and the adjoining bathroom full of flowers and parcels he took a horrified look and said, 'Are you starting a florist's shop? Where on earth are you going?' I replied, 'Actually to Lagos in Nigeria.' He then launched into an account of his horrifying experiences off the west coast of Africa during the war years. These included being torpedoed off Freetown in Sierra Leone. I was wonderfully treated on the ship as everyone decided I was going to 'the white man's grave.' The other passengers leaving the ship at Cape Town were going to various countries in East Africa which seemed to have a more salubrious reputation.

When the *Corinthic* was due to dock in Cape Town I determined to rise early to get a good view of the city as we entered the harbour. When my sister and I were young our father had told us that it was one of the most beautiful approaches in the world. He had not exaggerated. In the early dawn the harbour, the city and the wonderful backdrop of Table Mountain all looked incredibly beautiful.

Chapter 2

My Arrival in Africa

As soon as the company's agent had installed me at the Settlers Club and made arrangements for my onward passage to Lagos I made a sentimental journey to the Standard Bank in Adderley Street. My father was on the staff of this bank as a young man. Later he was delighted to hear that I had cashed a cheque at the same counter as he had worked from many years previously.

The next matter demanding urgent attention was the yellow fever injection. I finally located the department and joined a long queue of people, the majority of whom were going to South America. By the time I received this injection I was beginning to feel like an animated sieve. Fortunately the yellow fever injection did not have the same drastic after-effects as the typhoid-typhus.

After this I decided to do a little sightseeing around Cape Town. My first trip was by cable car to the top of Table Mountain. The car was only a few feet off the ground when I realized that the whole idea was a grave mistake. I have always had a very poor head for heights, and while the other occupants of the car were leaning out of the windows and going into raptures over the views I was sitting on the floor praying for the journey to end. The view from the mountain top was more impressive, but most of the time I was thinking about the return trip in the cable car. Since then I have admired the glories of the European Alps, the Himalayas, the Rockies and the New Zealand Alps either from ground level or as far as a motor car could take me. Strange to say I never had this feeling of nausea and giddiness when I was travelling in an aeroplane.

After two or three days sightseeing I embarked on the *Calabar* for Lagos. The *Calabar*, a small ship of the Elder-Demster line was no *Corinthic*. We were a mixed bag of passengers, government officials, mining personnel, missionaries, traders and a university lecturer and his wife. The captain looked after us well, and in spite of the diversity of nationality, language and occupation of the passengers we had a happy trip with the usual fun and games as we crossed the equator.

Quite the most amazing person on the ship was the doctor. He looked about sixty years old but the captain said he was over eighty. He had led an adventurous life as, apart from serving in the Boer War, the Great War and the Zululand native rebellion, he had travelled most of the world as ship's surgeon. Many years later a friend on the Nigerian Plateau told me that a ship on which her mother was travelling was wrecked off the inhospitable Skeleton Coast of West Africa. This doctor was the ship's surgeon and apart from his professional skills he did much to help the survivors although at this time he was the oldest member of the wrecked party. He also did an excellent job of looking after the passengers and crew on our voyage to Lagos.

Another interesting character on the ship was the radio operator. He kept a parrot for company, and one morning I received quite a shock when I saw the bird. At first I thought it was an Australian galah, but on closer inspection I discovered that it was a smaller bird, grey, with bright reddish pink tail feathers, but unlike the galah, no coloured feathers on the breast or head. It was a West African grey parrot. These birds are wonderful talkers and years later we kept one as a pet. This bird developed an amazing vocabulary. One of our African friends also told me that the tail feathers were often seen for sale on ju-ju medicine stalls in Yoruba markets.

After eight days at sea I obtained my first view of West Africa when I saw the outline of Takoradi through a haze and I must admit that it was a terrible disappointment. The sea was dark, oily and positively smelt. There was none of the lush tropical vegetation and colour that I had been used to seeing in the beautiful Pacific islands of Fiji, Western Samoa and Lord Howe Island. Several of the ship's passengers disembarked at Takoradi as they were going by road to Accra. Among those disembarking was my friend Mr Reid. He was manager of Cadbury's in Accra. We had played deck games together, mainly because I was not particularly skilled at deck games and the rest of the passengers were not too keen to have me as a partner. Mr Reed did not mind at all. He was extremely fat and it was my job to do anything which entailed bending, so I picked up all the darts and quoits for him. When he was leaving the ship he told me that if I got off the ship at Accra he would send his car and driver to show me around the city. I must admit that at that time I did not expect to be met by a chaffeur driven Rolls Royce. I felt distinctly honoured.

After the disembarkation formalities were completed a few of us went down to inspect the local market. This was a very colourful scene, with some of the women dressed in gay coloured cloth and wearing beautiful gold ornamental necklaces, bracelets and earrings. The whole scene was very bright and interesting. The local people's carriage was superb due to their carrying almost everything on their heads even large trays of pineapples, pawpaws, yams, bananas and coconuts.

A good deal of the market gave me something of a culture shock: vultures on a rubbish dump, tin trays of crawling crabs and entrails covered with flies, with children running around in the middle of it all. Some of the stall holders were even asleep among their wares.

The local native curio shop was very interesting with some beautiful gold filigree jewellery as well as ivory and wood carvings and elephant tables.

In the evening we had a pleasant diversion as most of the remaining passengers went to a picture show. It was held in an open air theatre. The film was an American one of ancient vintage, but most of the fun was off the screen. In the middle of the film I thought that a railway train had left the rails and crashed into the back of the theatre. The train passed at the immediate rear of the theatre and the driver stopped the engine where he could get a good view of the film. When he tired of it he restarted the train with much whistling and din. Twice during the show it started to rain heavily and we all had to rush for cover. I enjoyed the whole performance very much.

Next morning we anchored off Accra. In the distance it looked much more attractive than Takoradi and I was anxious to go ashore. Dozens of surf boats manned by Kru boatmen made it faintly reminiscent of the South Seas. At first it was thought to be too rough to disembark but after breakfast the agent said it would be all right so three of us braved it. I was young and active and after having made somewhat precarious landings on Lord Howe and Norfolk Islands was prepared for what followed. We were slung over the ship's side in a mammy chair and suspended over the surf boat. The boatman waited until he was in the trough of a wave and at this point we were dumped into the bottom of the boat. At this stage the Kru men took over and started to row us ashore. As the boat approached the shore you had to be pretty lively getting out without being soaked.

I believe that in earlier days the women were carried by the boatmen, but I decided to do it under my own steam and got drenched to the skin in the process. This was no hardship as the heat on shore was like stepping into an oven. I soon dried out and, looking a bit like Monday's unironed washing, went to call on Mr Reed. He generously put his magnificent car and his driver at our disposal. As a result we had an interesting tour of Accra including a call at Christiansborg Castle, the old Danish castle-cum-fort which was originally built in 1610 in the slave trading days. At the time of our visit it was the Governor's residence.

Other places of interest were the Achimota University and the hospital. As we travelled it became hotter and hotter, but at the end of the trip Mr Reed entertained us at his bungalow and provided us with cool soft drinks and iced beer, and after he had presented us with tins of Cadbury's chocolates we returned to the surf boat and back to the ship. Halfway between the shore and the ship the Kru boatmen decided to increase our fare. As the water was shark infested and it was a long swim in either direction we did not think that we were in any position to argue. We paid up and made it back to the ship and were hoisted aboard in the mammy chair. It had been a wonderfully interesting day.

We left for Lagos that evening and arrived there about 4.30 p.m. the following day. We had to await the arrival of the pilot and as a result it was almost dark when we docked.

As it was impossible for Tony to travel over seven hundred miles to meet me and as I knew no one in Lagos I was entirely dependent on information sent me that I would be met by an African, Mr Shoda, who would help me through the customs and immigration and take me to an hotel where I was to stay while awaiting my departure by train for Jos. By the time most of the passengers had disembarked there was no sign of Mr Shoda so I asked if I could remain on board until the following morning. However, as the captain had gone ashore I was told that it was against maritime regulations for me to remain on the ship.

I was just beginning to feel rather desperate and was wondering whether I should get in touch with the British Consul or spend the night sitting on the wharf, when a small, very dark man with a bright smiling, face arrived. He announced that he was Mr Shoda. He apologized for his lateness and explained that he was given incorrect instructions regarding my arrival. However, I was so glad to see him that I scarcely listened to his apologies. Thanks to Mr Shoda I had little difficulty with the customs and immigration. After the formalities were completed we got into a car and made for the old Bristol Hotel.

Looking back later, I have felt that it was a good thing that the journey was made in the dark as the surroundings were far from salubrious. When we arrived at the hotel there was not exactly 'Welcome' on the mat. Even in the dim light of the entrance the place looked pretty dreadful. Mr Shoda told me that at that time it was one of the best hotels in Lagos. I did not voice the sentiment that I would have hated to have seen the worst.

As we could not find the management I reverted to the custom of my earlier days in outback Australia by looking up the register and hopefully finding a vacant room. Mr Shoda said that he would inspect the room to see that everything was in order. It was better furnished than I had expected.

After Mr Shoda had departed I started to unpack. I decided to dispense with the bed linen and encased the pillow in my petticoat. At this stage I remembered my cousin's gift of the Insectibane. I finally located it and dusted it liberally around the bed. At least I thought I would not be troubled by fleas.

I slept well and was only awakened by a sound that I was to become very used to over the next eighteen years, the calling of the faithful to prayer. I then had a good look out of the bedroom window, and found that most of the views were rather sordid. However, in the courtyard of a building across the road there was a tame monkey and I had great fun watching its antics.

In the afternoon Mr Shoda took me for a drive around Lagos. Our first stop was the cable station as I knew my family would be getting worried about my whereabouts as I had had no means of communicating with them since I left Cape Town. The following morning I had to catch the train for Jos. We set off for Iddo Junction railway station. When we arrived there the bedlam was unspeakable, hundreds milling in all directions and every known human activity going on. Mr Shoda endeavoured to cut a swathe through some of the crowd, while I used some of my hockey playing tactics to certain advantage. Finally we made the railway carriage.

When the time came to say goodbye to Mr Shoda I felt that I was farewelling an old friend. In a certain sense I was, as the friendship lasted for the seventeen years that I travelled by train from Lagos to Jos. It covered two generations, for when the father gave up the job for the company his son took over. Without him my arrival in Lagos would have been much more painful and difficult, and I felt that I would never have made the up country train to Jos without his help.

The train left Iddo Junction on time and the seven hundred and thirteen mile journey was to prove very interesting. It covered a wide variety of scenery. As it was then approaching the end of the rainy season the country looked green and lush. There were numerous native farms, mainly sugar cane, corn, cocoa, oil palms and cassava. The journey was slow and we stopped at the many small stations serving various small towns and villages. Long stops were made at the large cities of Ibadan and Ilorin. At all stations a brisk trade was done with local vendors of all manner of things, but predominantly fruit and vegetables. This brisk trade in fruit, particularly pineapples and pawpaws produced a very pleasant bonus for me. The railway attendant from the dining car brought me some delicious fruit salad for afternoon tea.

On the second day out we crossed the Niger river. At the end of the rains it was truly magnificent sight. As I gazed at this mighty stream from the carriage window my mind went back to my school days when virtually the only thing any of the students knew about Nigeria was from the poem 'The Slave's Dream' with its reference to 'the lordly Niger.' I was a little more knowledgeable than some because as honours geography student I had made a study of the great river systems of the world. The curriculum put the main emphasis on the Nile, the Ganges and the Mississippi, but there was also reference to the Amazon, the Congo, and the Niger.

I was interested in the history and particularly in the exploration of these rivers, although I must admit that my main interest in Mungo Park derived from his extraordinary name. Whether the slave was dreaming of the Niger I will never know, but little did I dream as a student, that one day I would see the lordly Niger and later meet a man who had travelled on an exploratory trip on the Amazon.

This great river, the third largest in Africa after the Nile and the Congo, was certainly an impressive sight. Probably no river in the world was the source of so much controversy as to where its final outlet actually was. Although mention of this stream was made many centuries ago by Herodotus and vague references to it were made by Pliny and Ptolemy it was not until near the end of the eighteenth century that it was suspected that its outlet was into the Gulf of Guinea.

In the intervening centuries almost every conceivable theory had been advanced as to the source, the course and the outlet of the Niger. A popular theory in the Middle Ages was that there was a common source for the Nile and the Niger, and that the Niger, Benue and Senegal rivers formed one great river system flowing to the west and into the Atlantic.

When this theory was disproved other explorers including Leo Africanus (who probably sailed on a section of the Niger) still concluded that it flowed westward and it was shown this way on maps during the sixteenth, seventeenth and eighteenth centuries.

The German explorer Hornemann probably lost his life somewhere in Nigeria and Mungo Park, who travelled inland from the Gambia and reached the Niger at the Segou, established the fact that it flowed eastward and not westward. On his second journey in 1805 he determined to make the journey downstream to find the outlet, but unfortunately, as far as was known, he was drowned in the rapids at Bussa. Park always had the erroneous idea that the Niger joined the Congo.

The final evidence that it entered the sea at the Gulf of Guinea came in 1830 when Richard Lander, who had earlier been in the expedition led by Clappertown, returned to Africa and with his brother made the journey by canoe from Bussa to Brassal at the mouth of the Niger Delta.

However, after all these theories and explorations, the Niger never became the great trading river that was expected because it was not navigable from its entire length. The train driver obligingly stopped on the middle of the bridge so that we could get a better view of the river. The country through which we now travelled for many miles was known as Orchard bush. It was much more open than the heavily vegetated region out of Lagos and as I peered through the window of the train I hoped to see some big game animals. I was disappointed.

About 8.30 p.m. we arrived at Kaduna Junction where most of the passengers left the train. It was raining and there was unspeakable bedlam going on at the station. I was somewhat amazed when the train steward came into the carriage bearing blankets. Later in the night, in spite of the blankets I felt quite cold, and as the train was travelling very slowly I realized that we were making a steep ascent to a much higher elevation. In the morning I awakened to a different world. Apart from being much cooler the countryside was more sparsely vegetated, and there were large herds of Fulani cattle being driven across the country. These were strange hump-backed beasts with large horns. Finally I reached my destination, Bukuru station.

'Small Barn' – one of the Plateau's pleasant homes.

Chapter 3

My Arrival on the Plateau

When I stepped out of the train I thought that I must have arrived at the wrong place as there was practically no sign of life. I sat on my suitcase hoping like Mr Micawber that something would turn up. One thing which immediately intrigued me was the large number of gum trees growing around the station. These Australian trees made me feel a little less lonely, and it was not until months later that I discovered that the first General Manager of the company had come from Tasmania and had planted the trees to remind him of his native land.

Eventually, in a cloud of dust, Tony arrived at the station driving a landrover. He told me later that as the train never arrived on time he had been advised about half an hour before the official arrival time that there was no hurry and was having a leisurely beer in a friend's home when he heard the train whistle, and realized that for once the train was going to arrive at the correct time. After a cup of tea at the friend's house we set out for South Ropp where Tony was working at that time. It was a journey of some thirty-five miles and I think it was then that I fell in love with Nigeria.

It was to be an abiding love affair. The countryside looked beautiful, fresh and green with masses of golden coreopsis in flower over extensive flat plains which Tony had told me were old volcanic lava plains; blue hills some miles away, washed clean by the recent rains formed a spectacular background. The birds were a delight and the Hausa men in their colourful rigas were a pleasing sight. I learned that this was their normal attire, not something got up for tourists.

Our house at South Ropp was made of mud, with a thatched roof. It was whitewashed and painted with a black trim. It was basic, but comfortable inside and I soon started to visualize improvements. We did not have any close neighbours but that did not worry us as we had both lived in lonely parts of Australia.

I was enjoying the new experiences and surroundings very much and was making plans for a garden when Tony made the announcement, 'We are not going to be living here so don't get too involved, we are going bush as soon as this rainy season is over.' Where we were living looked pretty much bush to me. It could hardly be mistaken for Piccadilly Circus or Pitt St. in Sydney during a rush hour. Then he replied, 'This is different, we will be on trek,' and went on to explain that during the first part of our journey we would be travelling through various villages, from one rest house to the next, and when we reached the area that had to be explored and prospected we would set up a more permanent camp.

As I had always detested camping I asked how long this trek was likely to last and to my amazement I found that it was to last all through the dry season and until the beginning of the rains, about six months. The chief geologist, John Farrington, was anxious that the various members of the expedition would get away as soon as the rains were over. This left us with very little time to prepare. With such a short time at our disposal and in my case being quite unfamiliar with the ways of the country, getting gear ready for this bush tour was not easy.

We had to take out food, clothing, tents, bed linen, blankets, mosquito nets, guns, ammunition, chairs, tables, a portable bath, water filters, crockery, kitchen equipment, kerosene, tools, Tilley lamps, lamp mantles, hurricane lanterns, stretchers, geological equipment, a bicycle, tyres and a host of sundries too numerous to mention.

As Tony had been on trek during the previous dry season, and had experience of bush conditions he assumed responsibility for the geological, survey and mining equipment, guns and ammunition while I looked after food, clothing, household and personal effects. Regarding the latter I had been told to keep my wardrobe to a bare minimum, and to say that I travelled light was an understatement.

We had to take out a two months' supply of food and hopefully after that supplies would be sent out from company headquarters and somehow or other carried by porters to our camp.

An inspection of our company's canteen revealed that supplies of basic foodstuffs – flour, yeast, sugar, salt, coffee and tea were in plentiful supply as well as reasonable supplies of canned meat, fish, jams, fruit and even canned beer. Cleaning articles such as soap, disinfectants, water purifying tablets and several additions to the first aid box were added to the list as well as small amounts of luxuries such as chocolates, biscuits, fruit juices, liquor and the inevitable cornflakes.

Our next worry was the matter of the horses – Cobber, a small pagan pony and Tony's horse, Phar Lap. During the previous tour Tony had lost a horse through sleeping sickness. As we would be going through tsetse fly country again it was decided to take the horses to the veterinary research station at Vom for inoculation. While we were there the vet said that they now had a serum for human beings and he advised us both to have the injection before we returned to tsetse fly country. This necessitated a trip to the doctor in Jos. He asked why we needed the injection as the Plateau was not a sleeping sickness area.

He was horrified when I told him that I was going out on trek for six months, and said that the company was crazy for sending me and that I was crazy for going. I did point out that I did not have much choice. The company had no house for me to live in and, as I had left Australia to be with Tony, the bush it had to be. Anyway, he was very kind and told me to be sure to boil and filter all drinking water, to take anti-malaria tablets daily, never to sleep without a mosquito net and to hope for the best.

Tony and I had always been great animal lovers so decided that as we were going to be away for so long that we would take a kitten with us. He was a dear little black puss and we named him Ned Kelly after a notorious Australian bush ranger. The name proved apt for when Ned developed into a full grown cat he did become something of a bush ranger. With all the stuff we had to take with us our friends thought we were mad to be taking a cat as well, but Ned proved to be wonderful company for us and was very popular with the younger African boys and the domestic staff.

My next worry was the matter of communication with my relatives, I had promised to keep in the closest possible touch, something that was going to be virtually impossible if I was to be on trek in the Nigerian bush miles and miles from a post office and dependent on the irregular arrival of our stores for someone to take back mail to the Plateau for posting. The only thing I could do was to write a number of letters and give them to a friend to post to Australia at fortnightly intervals. Years later my sister said she had received very odd letters from me when I first went to Nigeria but concluded that I had gone 'Troppo', an Australian slang term for being somewhat out of one's mind when living in the tropics. Later she admitted that it must have been rather difficult to write letters in advance.

Chapter 4

On Trek

During the first week in October the rainy season had officially ended and the first Tuesday in October was the date selected for the start of the dry season's six months exploration. When any likely or promising area was discovered we then had to set up a more permanent camp and do more intensive exploration of the area. During the previous season Tony had discovered an area in the Bauchi Emirate which showed some promise so it had been decided that our first camp would be established in this region.

When everything was finally ready it certainly was a motley cavalcade which set out. We had two three-ton trucks loaded with mining and scientific gear, plus African labourers, their wives and miscellaneous belongings. Tony, Bob Hurley and I travelled in two kit-cars with our personal possessions, food stores and the more valuable equipment. Our first stop was to be at Bauchi. We left the Plateau early in the morning and because of the 4,000 feet of elevation it was quite cool. After leaving Jos we travelled by way of the Rafin Jaki escarpment. The scenery was most impressive particularly at Panshanu Pass, mountainous with luxuriant vegetation and the backdrop of the Dass Hills. By the time we reached Bauchi we had descended more than two thousand feet and the weather was much hotter. After lunch at Bauchi we set out for Alkaleri and this was my first experience of the Nigerian rest house.

We had just started to unpack when a messenger arrived with a dash of poultry, groundnut oil, tomatoes and onions. Next to arrive was the local Sarki or chief who was accompanied by one of his retainers carrying a mat and other items for his comfort. The mat was placed on the ground and after the Sarki was seated the 'magana' was commenced. His 'magana', or talk, was to be the forerunner of many more. Generally the routine was the same. First of all there would be polite enquiries regarding our health and

16

The Rest House at Alkaleri.

our work and then the presentation of the dash, usually one or two chickens, a few eggs or a green pawpaw and onions. Later, if available, rocks or mineral specimens would be brought out for inspection by Tony and questions would be asked as to where the specimens had been obtained. Then it would be our turn to make enquiries regarding their health and families and then Tony presented our dash, generally salt, tea, sugar, sweets, soap or canned goods.

After the sarki had departed we had our evening meal and I decided that it was time for bed. I was just about to get into bed when Tony shouted, 'Never get into bed in any of these rest houses without turning back the clothes to make sure there is not a snake in the bed!' With this bit of information I not only turned back the clothes, I virtually dismantled the bed.

For the remainder of my long sojourn in Nigeria I carefully inspected beds and always placed my slippers under the mosquito net. Even to this day, years after I have left Africa, I often unconsciously look in my shoes to make sure that there are no spiders or scorpions in them.

Early the next morning we set out for Gombe. On arrival there we called on the local district officer and then Tony had his magana with the sarki. We were anxious to get news of the rest of our cavalcade. The lorries had not been sighted since we left Jos so a good deal of time was spent in trying to locate them. All kinds of conflicting reports reached us, but finally someone came up with the information that they had passed through Gombe. Now we had to set off after them. I was nursing Ned Kelly and the excitement proved too much for him and he urinated all over my dress, so with heat, dust and cat pee I did not look or feel like something just out of *Vogue*! We hoped to reach Biliri before dusk, but the road, or more accurately, the bush track, was fast deteriorating. The scenery was remarkable, numerous volcanic peaks dominated by the towering Kaltunga. The whole scene looked like a fitting backdrop to the film *The Lost World*. By this time we had located the lorries.

Just as the sun was setting we were fording a creek when Bob Hurley's truck became bogged, and in trying to go around him ours followed suit. Further back along the track the lorries suffered the same fate. Everything had to be unloaded from the vehicles and placed beside the track so that the kit-cars could be 'debogged' and moved forward. In the midst of the excitement Ned Kelly had had enough and shot off into the long grass. He was later located by one of the Africans. I was rushing around trying to 'make do' to ensure that our flour, tea and sugar were not being ruined by the downpour.

By this time I was resigned to spending the night in a deck chair in the back of our kit-car, serving as the main course in a feast for myriads of mosquitoes. The men were trying to move the trucks with not much success but just when things were at their worst we were rescued by an American missionary, the Revd. Walter Erbele of the Sudan United Mission. Not only was he the spiritual leader of the smaller village of Filiya, but he also looked after their material needs, their education, their health, their correct farming and the maintenance of their tools and so on. Walter Erbele and his wife Ruth represented the finest type of pioneer missionary, and although it later became fashionable to sneer at missionary work in Africa I can only say that I found these people of all denominations the salt of the earth. They worked in lonely unhealthy situations for practically no money and every village that I saw which had a missionary was greatly improved by their presence.

Walter and Ruth looked after me, Tony and Bob Hurley for three days while we sorted out our belongings. The motor vehicles were prepared for return to the Plateau and so departed our last link with civilization. We now had to do it the hard way mostly on the flat of our feet. We set out at dawn for our first stop, a village named Gidan Deri nine miles distant. We looked a strange crowd.

The carriers set off first with the head loads and the rest followed in single file along the narrow track. Tony usually headed the column with his gun bearer bearing two rifles, heavy bore for big animals such as

Gabriel Ladele and Musa Kano cutting a track through the elephant grass.

antelope and a .22 for smaller game and birds. We and the labourers depended on Tony's rifles to keep us supplied with extra rations of meat. I followed, carrying my survival kit: boiled water for drinking, the first aid box, and my cosmetic bag. I also tried to cope with Ned Kelly. He proved to be very obstreperous and had to be passed from person to person. Even in the early morning it was very hot with the elephant grass growing about eight feet high on either side of the track. The trek as measured by the cyclometer wheel proved to be nearer ten miles than nine and it felt to me more like a hundred.

I felt sorry for the labourers with their heavy loads. It was not long before I was bringing up the rear of the procession and on glancing back I nearly had a heart attack as, just at the back of me, were two stark naked men armed with large bows and arrows. In spite of the heat I did a bit of queue jumping and hurried up to Tony. He said our naked companions were hunter men and as such were very skilled at stalking prey. They were adept at moving noiselessly and had probably been following us for miles.

Just before we reached Gidan Deri we were met by the 'doki' boys with our dokis or horses. The poor brutes looked thin and not at all like the lovely horses that left the plateau. Cobber had a big sore on his back and I rather suspected that the money intended to provide corn for the horses had been spent on other things. The two horse blankets had also disappeared.

We finally reached Gidan Deri and another rest house. These circular mud walled structures got progressively worse as we progressed. This looked particularly verminous but at least it was only for two or three nights. We were just getting installed when the local sarki arrived. He was a colourful character named Borodi. He was decked out in considerable finery and had a leopard skin spread over his horse. He was a Fulani. The Fulani are a mysterious race whose origin has never been solved, although several theories have been advanced, one suggestion even being that they were the descendants of the Philistines referred to in the Bible. They were scattered over various parts of West Africa, but the largest number were found in the northern provinces of Nigeria. They were divided into two groups, the town Fulani and the cattle Fulani. Unlike the town Fulani the cattle Fulani rarely intermarried with other races and as a result kept their racial characteristics much less diluted than the town Fulani. Most of them had coppery coloured complexions, but in some of the more remote places were almost fair, I remember seeing one man at a small market in the Bauchi Emirate who had a fairer skin than many Europeans.

The cattle Fulani were well named as their whole life revolved around their large herds of hump-backed cattle. They were a nomadic people and spent their lives wandering all over the country looking for food and water for their animals. The cattle were usually under the care of young boys whose clothing consisted of a goatskin wound around the waist and over one shoulder and each carried a long thin wooden staff. There was a tremendous rapport between the boys and their cattle. They talked to them and played them tunes on their reed pipes.

Strange to say, years later in Greece I saw a very similar scene, only this time it was a shepherd boy with a crook playing a tune to a small flock of sheep.

Being nomads the cattle Fulani had no permanent homes and camped wherever there were food and water for their stock. Their homes were very basic, probably the original pre-fabs or mobile houses. They were made from long canes which they bent over to make a framework for their house. The frame was then covered with reeds, grass, zana mats, or whatever material was available. When the time came to shift camp they just pulled up the canes and transported them along with all their household goods piled on the backs of their cattle. This way they were easily transported.

The women of the tribe seemed to do a great deal of the work, making butter, cheese and muddera, a milk dish similar to yoghurt. These products were carried to local markets by the women and sold. The women's dress was simple – a skirt wrapped around them after the style of a Pacific pareu. They spent a good deal of their time dressing their long black hair. It was generally braided into plaits and frequently ornamented with genuine gold ornaments. They also wore a considerable amount of jewellery – earrings, bracelets, and rings. Their main diet was milk and milk products. They ate very little meat but sometimes mixed a type of porridge with blood. Whether it was their diet or their nomadic life entailing miles of walking I don't know, but both men and women were consistently the thinnest people I have ever known. I never remember seeing a fat man, woman or child.

Borodi was a town Fulani and like many of his race highly intelligent. When young he had been a slave in the household of the local sarki. He had evidently been very well treated and accepted as a member of the family. Like many of the town Fulani he held down a good position in his village. Strange to say many of the town Fulani were the local tax collectors. This profession can hardly have endeared them to their brothers, the cattle Fulani, as the cattle Fulani were taxed on the number of cattle in their herds, and on large herds the tax was considerable. However tax evasion was not unknown and the head count was rather elastic as cattle just seemed to vanish when the tax gatherer was around.

One aspect of Fulani life in which I was determined to take no part was the initiation ceremony of young boys into manhood. It was known as Sheriya or Fulani Beating and although outlawed by government in the nineteen fifties it was fairly common in the more remote areas when we were in the bush. All of the local villagers turned out for these ceremonies. One film which I saw of the beatings made me quite ill and I was very glad that I had not witnessed the actual beating. Prior to the ceremony the initiates fast and abstain from sexual intercourse.

Until they have passed this initiation they have no hope of acquiring a wife as the beating and the resultant scars prove they were brave and manly.

For the actual beating the spectators sat around in a circle. The young Fulani girls were dressed in their best clothes and wore their gold ornaments. The initiates were brought into the centre of the circle and as they wore only a loin cloth they had no clothing for protection. One of the boys was selected and another young man, often an initiate from the previous year, faced him. He had a long staff and with this he started to flog his victim most brutally. The flogged youth could not flinch or show any signs of pain. The floggings left terrible scars, but they were worn as a mark of distinction, and I suppose carried the same prestige as the sabre cuts inflicted on cadets in certain German universities. Sadly many of the boys were seriously wounded and quite a few died of blood poisoning from the dreadful wounds inflicted at the sheriya.

After the usual magana and exchange of gifts Borodi intimated that he would like to have his photo taken and that he would be back next day with his wives. He duly arrived next morning with his two wives decked out in their best finery. After the photography session we checked and packed our gear so that we could make an early start next morning on what I fervently hoped would be our last day of trekking for a few weeks.

We started for Diji just after dawn. As usual the carriers with the head loads started first. Ned Kelly had to become a head load as he had become too much of a nuisance to be carried in arms. Ned was unceremoniously locked into a chop box, and loaded on to the head of Ali Bashar, a very likeable lad of about fifteen. Ali was delighted as Ned was a light load. The chickens had to go into a makeshift cage and also became a head load. The trek was only about six miles but far enough on foot with the day getting hotter every mile. Eventually we reached Diji.

Chapter 5

The Camp at Diji

As our camp at Diji was to be of a semi-permanent nature it had to be more comfortable than the rest houses, tents and temporary establishments which we had suffered on trek. As it was getting hotter a site was chosen under the shade of a large tree. Frenzied activity followed. The first things that had to be made were the zana mats. These mats made from elephant grass formed the walls of the living-cum-dining room. The sleeping tents furnished with canvas stretchers and mosquito nets were placed at either end of the living room. The roof of the living area was then roughly thatched with zana mats and lined with a green canvas tarpaulin. This gave us a comparatively cool area in which to sleep or shelter from the heat of the sun. We had two folding canvas chairs and two deck chairs fitted with head pillows. The table was of a folding variety to make it more convenient for carrying. At the back of my tent was a bathroom made from zana matting. In this we put our portable bath, one of our greatest blessings. It was an enamel bath fitted into a wicker basket and equipped with a lid. On trek it made a convenient head load as many of our lighter odds and ends including our bed linen and towels were loaded into it. I believe that at one time these baths were standard issue for government officials in Nigeria, but were later replaced with canvas folding baths.

At the back of Tony's tent there was a zana mat store room in which tin trunks and the more valuable items were stored. Guns and money were also usually kept there.

Our biggest problem at this camp was dust. As soon as possible I managed to get some light woven mats from the village market and these placed on the earthen floor made life much more pleasant. Mats were a wonderful standby in Nigerian life, as they were used for prayer mats,

23

A temporary bush camp.

sleeping mats, floor coverings and as carry-alls wrapped around a motley collection of goods. The Fulani cattlemen even used them as rain capes in the rainy season. Two joined together and worn something like a small tent were known as a kapeta.

Our arrival created great excitement in the village. I was the first white woman many of the villagers had seen. Their reactions were a bit mixed. Tony said it was great, as he had little difficulty hiring labourers while I was with him as many turned up out of curiosity. Most of the small children, after one look at me, usually started yelling. This was not exactly flattering, but I consoled myself with the thought that the most glamorous film star would probably have produced the same reaction. I have no doubt that the mothers disciplined their children by telling them that they would be given to the 'white witch' if they misbehaved.

Tony left early next morning as he had a great deal of work to do. His first consideration in setting up any permanent camp was to select a site where water was likely to be obtained. Apart from providing a supply of water for ourselves, new wells were a boon to the African villagers. I was fascinated by the method of well construction. The man digging it usually had to go down about thirty feet before water came to it. The well sinker never used a ladder but climbed up the almost perfectly straight sides by making small toe holds and then hanging on to these although there was practically nothing to hang on to.

One morning, while walking back from an inspection of the well, I noticed that our steward boy had managed to find a clothes prop. It was a hunting spear, so this was definitely the African version of 'beating swords into plough shares'. Throughout my many years in Nigeria I had always tried to encourage the use of clothes lines and props, admittedly with little success. Laundry was usually dried by spreading it on the ground or hanging it over bushes, and a horrible insect known as the Tumbo Fly laid its eggs on the warm laundry. When you wore your clothes or used the bed linen the young maggots would burrow into your skin and proceed to grow, eventually becoming a small worm. These were difficult to remove and if they died in the process would fester and cause infection. Fortunately these creatures were not a great problem during the dry season and as we had such a small amount of clothing and linen I always made sure it was well ironed and dried under a mosquito net.

About this time Tony began to complain of a sore leg, but we did not take much notice thinking that it was probably caused by a scratch which he had got scrambling in and out of the trenches. As the pain became increasingly worse we decided that it was a boil and treated it accordingly. We did not anticipate the worry, pain and trouble that was ahead of us. Now that we had settled in we began to think about Bob Hurley. His camp was about six miles from ours and was in an even lonelier situation. He had impressed on his labourers that if anything happened to him that they were to come over and contact us right away. As he was trenching and sinking a shaft it was somewhat worrying, but Bob had worked all over the world and was a very competent miner and prospector. I decided that as we had an official holiday over Christmas he could come over to our camp and we could have Christmas together.

Once the initial worries of establishing the camp were over we settled into our daily routine. After an early breakfast Tony left for work at about 7 a.m. It was an early start for a long day but a large amount of work had to be done during the dry season, so anything like a forty hour, five day week was something we had only heard about. After he left I conducted my sick parade. I was not a trained nurse, but I had done a first aid course and I had worked in a psychiatric hospital for three months so had some knowledge of the basics. Unfortunately there was much that I could do nothing about so these cases had to be left to the local medicine man. The luckier ones could get treatment at the nearest mission dispensary if they could walk or get transport, but as we were in such a remote area this was usually impossible for them so I just had to do what I could. Most of my cases were rudimentary – sore eyes, cuts, sprains, head lice, boils, malaria and because of their diet, constipation or diarrhoea. I soon found that such sophisticated terms meant nothing to the villagers, labourers or our domestic staff, and I often wondered what my mother or some of my teachers would have thought if they had heard me asking African men if they 'shit small' or 'shit too much'!

After the sick parade was over I checked and distributed the day's ration of flour, sugar, salt, tea, coffee, cooking oil, etc. I had to keep a fairly rigorous check on stores as we did not know when or where the next supplies were likely to arrive. For the same reason daily menus had to be carefully planned.

In the late afternoon I always went for a walk and then came back and did my skipping exercises. The African children used to love to watch me skipping. I tried to teach them to skip, but very few mastered the art which I found rather strange as they were natural dancers and had a wonderful sense of rhythm, but they always seemed to hop at the wrong time and get entangled in the rope.

After our evening bath we always changed for dinner. Unlike some government officials we did not don full evening dress as our very limited wardrobe did not allow for such luxuries. I know that in this day of more casual dress many people find this dressing for dinner a ridiculous relic of old colonial days, but there was a very good reason for it. Apart from making one feel better it was good for morale, particularly in lonely camps and out stations where if there was any slackening of standards and too much drink it would not have been difficult to finish up like one of the more depraved characters in a Somerset Maugham story. Sometimes after dinner we would go down to the village to hear the drums and the singing and watch the dancing. Sometimes they would sing about us, and strangely we were always expected to pay a small amount for this privilege, a local dash.

They enjoyed watching me do the samba and our joint effort at barn dance they found hilarious. On other evenings we would do our reading and writing, insects permitting. I often said that Nigeria was an entomologist's paradise and a geologist's hell as there were times when the only way we could get free of insects was to take the Tilley lamp and fix a table up under a mosquito net. In one camp they became so bad that if we had soup at dinner the only way was to have our meal under a net or the whole meal was going to be enriched by the addition of protein we could well do without.

My next chore was to do something about the number of scrawny chickens we had accumulated as dashes from various village sarkis. I had also started a small garden. As we were approaching Christmas I thought some kind of pen could be made for the chickens. I would buy some local corn and fatten them up for the festive season. One of the African boys constructed a pen from thorn bushes and I hoped this would keep the chickens away from the small garden I proposed to start. Once the labourers had finished digging me a small patch I decided to plant quick growing things like radishes, lettuce, beans and tomatoes.

The chicken pen led to an incident which in retrospect was rather amusing, but at the time nearly scared the living daylights out of me. We had retired early but I could not sleep because of the bright moonlight, and as I turned over on my shoulder what did I see but a large spotted animal pacing around my mosquito net. I knew there were leopards in the area, and was petrified because I thought that if I awakened Tony out of a sound sleep and he grabbed a gun I was in more danger of being shot than of being mauled by a wild animal. Finally I plucked up courage and shouted to him, 'Don't shoot, but there is an animal in my tent!' The animal did one more course around the net and then disappeared outside.

I did not sleep much during the rest of the night, but in the morning the mystery was solved. A large spotted bush cat had discovered the chicken pen, and in chasing one of the chickens had dashed into our zana mat living room, and then into my tent. When later other geologists told me that bush animals never came near the tents I always had my doubts.

Tony, Audu, Umoru and Ned Kelly at Diji Camp.

Chapter 6

Christmas at Diji Camp

As Christmas approached I began to think that we were in for a very lean and lonely time. Our basic food supplies were dwindling fast and although Tony was able to supplement the larder by shooting the odd guinea fowl or sometimes a small antelope we were still very short of fresh vegetables and fruit. We managed to get onions from the local market and occasionally a green pawpaw. I used the latter in place of vegetable marrows and, stuffed with any available minced meat and rice, it made a change from the inevitable scrawny chicken.

However, just before Christmas we received definite 'manna from heaven.' Not only did our two months supply of basic rations and the long awaited mail arrive, but the company sent us a magnificent Christmas hamper. It contained a large Christmas cake, a pudding, two tins of chocolates, two tins of toffees, a beautiful tin of biscuits and three bottles of liquor, gin, whisky and brandy. About the same time our missionary friends Walter and Ruth Erbele sent over a large box of grapefruit, limes and tomatoes. As the two mission boys had walked several miles with this box they were rewarded with a Christmas gift and we were able to repay some of the kindness of the Erbeles by sending them a hamper from our stores.

On Christmas Eve Bob Hurley arrived with his stretcher, a large bunch of bananas and some Christmas fare from his hamper. While I was rushing around doing last minute preparations for next day's dinner I happened to mention that I had read somewhere that if ducks and chickens were given a drink of brandy prior to their execution the flesh would be more tender. Bob came up with the more intelligent suggestion that if we drank the brandy before the meal we would not notice if the birds were tough or not. The chicken and duck were duly dispatched without their drink of

28

brandy. As it was very hot at midday we decided to have our dinner in the evening.

Although none of the villagers and only one of our labourers was a Christian word soon spread that Christmas was a time for gift giving so early on Christmas morning there was a flurry of activity. Cigarettes, razors, handkerchiefs and sun glasses were given to our adult workers while children got sweets and biscuits. Josiah, our Christian labourer from Calabar, Southern Nigeria, then went for a walk to see if he could find some flowers, and something that would pass for festive greenery. By nightfall all was ready and after pre-dinner drinks we sat down to the best meal we had eaten since leaving the Plateau. I still have the menu as I wrote it:

CHRISTMAS DAY MENU

DIJI CAMP (Northern Nigeria)

Chicken Soup
Roast Duck and/or Roast Chicken
Baked Potatoes Baked Onions
Tinned Green Peas

Pawpaw with Tinned Cream
Christmas Pudding
Chocolates and Liqueurs

We lived on the memory for weeks

As we finished our drinks I thought few people could be spending a lonelier Christmas. Our thoughts turned to our families and friends in Australia, while Bob drank a toast to his wife and three children in Portugal.

After Christmas we soon settled back into routine. Bob Hurley returned to the mine and Tony and his labourers went back to work on the prospect trenches, patients at my sick parade continued to increase and more villagers, particularly the young people came to visit me. I was very interested in one lass who brought me a dash of sweet potatoes. She was wearing silver earrings and when I examined them closely I discovered they were old German coins. They were probably traded down through the Cameroons when it was a German colony. Other interesting visitors were two girls who looked almost white or off-white. As the girls were friends of Momo, our bush cook, I gathered that a liberal application of our flour contributed to the colour change in their complexion.

One morning I was sitting at the table typing when suddenly a European man walked through the door. I'll never know who got the greater surprise. He was the District Officer from Bauchi. When we had both recovered from our initial shock he said that some Africans had told him that a European man was working in the area, but he said that never in his wildest dreams had he expected to meet a European woman in such an isolated spot. It was a pleasant interlude to catch up on some of the news of the outside world.

My garden continued to flourish apart from the lettuces. These were finished off by some of the chickens but radishes, beans and tomatoes continued to be a welcome addition to our menu.

Just as everything appeared to be running smoothly the whole camp was thrown out of gear by something we had not anticipated. Tony now developed large carbuncles on his arms and legs and they became progressively worse. I knew the rudimentary treatment we had was practically useless, and if they became infected we were in for serious trouble. The last thing an exploration geologist needed was bad legs.

As the condition became much worse we decided that something would have to be done. A labourer was sent on trek to the Revd. Walter Erbele to see if he could give us directions to the nearest doctor or the nearest dispensary. When the answer came back we found that there was a dispensary at a place called Pero, and the only known doctor was a Doctor of Divinity at some mission station. Miserable and ill as Tony felt he said he hoped that he was not bad enough to require the services of a Doctor of Divinity, but decided that he would have to ride his horse to the dispensary at Pero.

This posed many problems. We could not pack up the entire camp and move to an area that had no bearing on the exploration work, nor could we leave this camp equipped as it was with scientific instruments, money, guns and gelignite. Finally we decided that Tony would go to Pero and I would remain behind to look after the camp. As I knew he would be away for at least four days and nights I put on a brave face and hoped for the best. Next morning he left for Pero. He looked very ill indeed, I bandaged his legs and hoped that the slow ride would not be too painful.

Back at the camp my first excitement was that our rather stupid horse boy had lost my little pony Cobber. After the concerted efforts of the headman Josiah, Audu, and half the village Cobber was located and returned to the camp. I decided that the horse boy would have to be found another job. As evening approached I decided that I must have been about the loneliest woman in the world. I made up my mind to sit up for most of the night. I had for company a French speaking night watchman from Fort Lamy. We lit a large fire to keep at bay any prowling hyenas, leopards, etc.

I certainly did not lack music, the night watchman had a native instrument, a molo, something like a one stringed lyre which he played and the village orchestra was putting on its best turn. I had never heard such concerted drumming and I wondered if they were celebrating a wedding or a festival. I did not think they had any designs on my safety as I was much too thin for the cooking pot. Next morning I sent the headman down to the village to find out what all the racket was about and they told him 'they knew madam would be frightened and they were drumming to keep the hyenas away.' I was deeply touched.

As Momo the cook had travelled with Tony I went out to the bush kitchen to prepare breakfast, only to discover that Audu, the steward had not only given him our bush stove but had also given him our bread, tin opener, and big knife as well. Fortunately I still had a saucepan or two and with an open fire managed to cope with my meals. Tony returned after four days. He looked a little better as the nursing sister at the dispensary had given him penicillin injections for the carbuncles. She did not hold out much hope of a rapid recovery as she herself was suffering from carbuncles and her predecessor had suffered from them during her entire four year tour.

We never found out what actually caused them or why they were so prevalent in this particular area. The sister had kindly provided Tony with some penicillin and hypodermic needles so I was able to continue the injections but the carbuncles never actually cleared up until we went on leave to England.

Just at this time we seemed to be plagued with ill health as our headman and a couple of labourers developed malaria. This we managed to treat but two of the village children died of what appeared to be meningitis which was very worrying as there was nothing we could do about it. Fortunately it did not develop into an epidemic.

About this time we went into the dental business. Momo came in one morning looking very miserable and complained that his tooth was aching 'too much'. Tony looked at it and said that as it appeared to be quite loose it would be a good idea to extract it. We had no proper dental appliances so we boiled up the pliers and, although Momo was a Muslim, he consented to swallowing a stiff dose of brandy. While Audu and I held Momo, Tony yanked out the tooth with one sharp tug and then gave the patient another shot of brandy. I thought that he would feel like murdering us but he was so delighted to have the tooth out that he told all his friends and soon after we had a queue of those wanting extractions. However, we were afraid of complications and infections and the would-be dental patients had to be content with clove oil and other temporary measures.

Eventually things calmed down and work was resumed at a feverish pace. The chief geologist, John Farrington, came down from the Plateau. He brought mail and stores and, as we had anticipated, told us that we would have to leave this prospect at the beginning of March and make our way down to join the base camp at Gwiwan Kogi. Although a great deal of trenching and prospecting had been done in our area there was very little tangible result. Small occurrences of lead ore had been discovered but not sufficient for any viable commercial enterprise. We now had a great deal of work to do before we could set out on trek again. Our main problem was to reduce the head load to a minimum. Borodi and his labourers took away the galena which had been mined during the trenching. They had a good local market for this.

A small amount was used as an eye shadow cosmetic after it was ground to a powder and called tozali. Following the ancient custom of the Egyptians and the modern fashion of Miss Elizabeth Arden the girls and some of the men outlined their eyelids with the tozali.

Bob Hurley had not finished his work and had to remain at his mine site after we left so we decided that we would have a farewell dinner at his camp prior to our departure. As we had to walk some miles over a rough bush track Tony set out with the Tilley lamp, some maps and charts for Bob, I followed carrying a bottle of liquor, while Audu brought up the rear with our crockery and cutlery. The dinner turned out to be the meal that never was. Bob was always very good company and time passed very pleasantly while we were chatting and drinking but when the meal had not materialized by 10 p.m. we thought it was time to investigate. I found Audu who said that there would be no dinner as Mr Hurley's kitchen had been burnt down. This was something of a disaster as apart from losing our meal most of our dishes had been lost in the fire. As we were very short of crockery I had visions of us eating out of calabashes until we reached our base camp.

A few days before leaving Tony had to visit Pai River so I decided to accompany him. The local sarki said that he would also come with us and brought his bows and arrows. I think his name should have been William Tell, as he was certainly a wizard with his weapons. It was not surprising that the early missionaries and traders had such a horror of bows and poisoned arrows. The hunters sneaked up so quietly that I should imagine that the first thing one would know of an attack would be when the arrow hit you.

On the way to Pai River we saw quite a few baboons and some small antelopes. Tony did not shoot any of the baboons as the Muslim labourers would not eat them and neither would I unless faced with utter starvation.

Tony and the Sarki each shot a small antelope so there was ample meat for the always meat hungry labourers. The country around Pai River was very attractive with a large number of palms growing along the water course. However it was low lying and I should imagine very unhealthy. While we were sitting in the shade having lunch we noticed a few tsetse flies around and were careful to avoid bites, as it was in this area in the previous year that Tony had lost his horse from sleeping sickness.

When we were ready to leave Diji for base camp at Gwiwan Kogi we anticipated several brief stops and camps before meeting the landrover which was to take us on the last stage of our journey. The last day at Diji was memorable. John Farrington left early to trek to the base camp and then return to the Plateau and Tony went over to Bob Hurley's camp to make a final check on the shaft. After lunch I decided to have a rest and must have fallen into a deep sleep to be suddenly awakened by a horrible roaring noise. I rushed out to see a positively terrifying sight, a fire rushing towards the camp from three directions. The only people at the camp were Audu the steward, a lame night watchman and myself. I rushed to the night watchman and practically dragged him to the enclosure and yelled at Audu to come over. At that moment I wondered if there was any gelignite in the pit. Thankfully there was not. We could never have got it out anyway. By this time the flames were getting close to the camp and the zana mat lavatory was ablaze and our portable lavatory was burnt. After the portable bath this item known colloquially as a 'thunderbox' was our most useful piece of equipment. By now I thought the whole camp would be burnt and I rushed to the lame guard and helped him to higher ground near the village. Here we waited, expecting our whole camp to go up in flames. Then, like a miracle, the wind dropped and we were able to beat out some of the remaining flames.

I learned later that serious as all bush fires are, the bush in Africa did not burn with the speed and intensity of the horrific fires in my homeland Australia where the volatile oils in the native vegetation can make everything a raging inferno in seconds.

I was not likely to forget my last day at Diji. When it was all over I found that my legs would not stop shaking. In the middle of the pandemonium one of the labourers came in with a small fawn which Tony had shot. Normally this would have been a big event but in the general confusion it passed almost unnoticed. Most of the head loads were packed and assembled in the evening so that we could start our trek as early as possible the next day.

Tony and the carriers set out first and the rest of us made up a rather motley procession not exactly in the best traditions of *Sanders Of The River*. Josiah, our English speaking Presbyterian, led our little troop. He had a cyclometer affixed to a bicycle wheel to measure the distance travelled. I followed carrying my survival kit, then Ladi the cook's wife with her pet lamb. She balanced the kettle on her head and carried the lamb in her arms for most of the journey. Next came young Ali Basher with Ned Kelly in a box as a head load. Ned protested loudly as he was never enthusiastic about this method of travel. Momo, our bush cook and the pony Cobber brought up the rear. The trek was six and a half miles and we did it in two hours exactly. It was a hideous walk as the grass had been burnt and we were all made filthy by the charcoal from the half burnt elephant grass as we pushed our way through it. We were very glad to reach our destination, Nahuta village. We did not feel clean until we had washed all the dust and soot off our bodies.

Preparations for lunch while on trek. Audu in foreground.

Chapter 7

The Camp at Nahuta

As we were supposed to be here for only a short time a temporary camp was established. It was a horrible situation, perched on the top of a rise and exposed to all the elements in the form of wind, dust, and dirt. However, it was the only available place at a reasonable distance from the village where there was a large shady tree. Our main worry was the water supply. There was no time to find a well watered situation and Tony had to set about getting a well sunk in a favourable area. Our first cup of tea tasted peculiar and I discovered that the water had been taken from a small pool full of leaves. Worse was to follow as I soon found that we were sharing our water supply with a herd of goats, and the local inhabitants including several lepers. It also served as the local laundry and bath house. Although we boiled and filtered all water I can't say that we really enjoyed it, either in tea or even when laced with orange squash or brandy.

Our first night's rest at the Nahuta camp was rudely interrupted by the arrival outside our tent of the wife of one of our labourers, stark naked and crying piteously. Adamu had just bought a new wife. She was a dear little girl, and Adamu was at least old enough to be her father. Naturally there had been trouble. She wanted to go back to her own country, Yala, but Adamu said that he had paid plenty money for her and to reinforce his argument had given the poor child a sound beating. During the night there was more trouble and Adamu put her out after taking all her clothes. My meagre wardrobe was practically non-existent but as her need was greater than mine I parted with one of my three blouses and a striped seersucker table cloth which would serve her as some kind of a makeshift skirt.

In the morning Tony sent for Sarkin Gwonna to try to get things sorted out. Finally they were settled, but not very happily. Adamu was very concerned about the financial angle and the loss of his money if the girl

The house at Nahuta – a truly dreadful spot.

Leaving our house at Nahuta wearing the pith helmet I said I would never wear.

went back to Yola. Tony said that if there was any more trouble they would both be sent back to the Plateau when we reached Base Camp.

The discovery of several small occurrences of lead ore at Nahuta made our stay much longer than we had anticipated. The weather was getting hotter and working conditions became more difficult so Frank Williams, the Assistant Chief Geologist, trekked over from Base Camp to spend a few days and supervise arrangements while I helped Tony with reports and other papers so that we would be able to get away more or less on schedule.

Frank thought it might be better if I travelled back to Bukuru by truck and then come back to Base Camp again by truck. This would have meant almost four hundred miles of hot, cramped sitting, over rough and dusty roads so I said that I would settle for seventy miles of hot walking.

One evening I walked over to Frank Williams' camp and noticed a very interesting tree growing at the side of the track. It had large seed pods about the size of pumpkin marrows hanging down from the branches. Tony said camps should not be placed under the shade of these trees as when he was in this area the previous year he had pitched his tent under one of them and during the night a pod had fallen off and shattered a wooden box underneath. The pods were very heavy and very hard. The tree had long trails of red flowers, deep reddish brown in colour and shaped rather like a gloxinia. This tree is related to the well known tulip tree and is, I have been told, a member of the Spathodea family.

When we were ready to leave Nahuta there were farewells all around. We were almost like old residents. First to arrive was Sarkin Kudu. He was a most colourful figure arrayed in a really gorgeous riga of parchment satin embroidered in brown and gold. His head-dress was a vivid scarlet. His farewell dash to me was a pet lamb and two green pawpaws. I gave him a gift of canned food and his photo.

It was rather strange seeing our headman Umoru, and steward Audu bowing on all fours in the dust before the sarki. He gave Umoru a fountain pen and said that he would shortly be returning to Gombe. I felt as if we were farewelling Vice-Royalty. Umoru later told me that Sarkin Kudu loved Master and Madame. I wondered if this made me a likely candidate for his harem.

In the meantime Frank Williams had gone over to inspect Bob Hurley's mine shaft. He brought Bob back with him for a farewell discussion and dinner. As most of the conversation was about lead, zinc, trenches, prospecting and chemical treatment of minerals I began to feel like a geological outcrop myself so retired early. Next morning Borodi and

A remote rest house. We lived in one round house, Bob Hurley lived in the other. We shared a community living-room.

Sarkin Kudu returned to say Goodbye again. After I had farewelled them and Frank Williams, Tony and I decided to start our packing before it got too hot. The following morning when we were ready to leave we discovered that we did not have enough carriers as the departure of Sarkin Kudu and Frank Williams had depleted our labour force. As a result we could not make an early start and half the loads had to be left behind. Consequently it was blazing hot before we started. I had to leave my pet lamb behind so made it a dash to Sarkin Nahuta.

After we left Nahuta we knew that there would be no more settled camps. We travelled as far as we could each day and pitched the tents in the coolest spot we could find. Although I was a good walker I could not travel as fast as the men. Our stop-overs were usually in isolated areas and there was a very little variety in the orchard bush country.

One interesting camp was at a place called Borokoto. It was in rocky country at the foot of the Gwonna Hills. Another geologist, Tom John, had camped there the previous year so there was no problem about selecting a camp site. The following morning we walked through the Gwonna Hills and saw many baboons. I had read that baboons sometimes threw rocks at anyone passing through their territory, but although they had plenty of ammunition they did not trouble us. We noticed that the Africans had set quite a number of animal traps, including a large leopard trap.

All of these traps were ingeniously constructed. While we were walking along we picked something which looked like wild plums. They were very good eating and much appreciated as it was quite a while since we had had any fresh fruit.

Our next campsite was a very pleasant one, but during the night a cyclone blew up. At about 2 a.m. Tony's tent fly fell down on him and unfortunately snapped the canes of his mosquito net. All the tent pegs blew out of my tent but the ridge pole remained secure so I spent the remainder of the night with everything flapping in every direction. The table with our breakfast dishes set out on it blew over and our limited supply of crockery was even further reduced.

We started just before dawn on what was to be the final stage of our journey before we reached base camp. We were to collect the landrover and the truck at Zurak. By this time the horses and the horse boys were with us again so after walking a few miles I mounted Cobber my pagan pony and jogged along in the heat. We had a hectic time keeping tsetse flies off the horses in the Pai River zone, as once again we were in tsetse fly area. When we reached the river the Africans tried to stop the horses from drinking. They knew that animals died near this river, but knowing nothing of tsetse fly infection, thought it was the water that caused the sickness.

Some of the carriers swam the river. It looked inviting but apart from the crocodiles I had no wish to contract the horrible disease bilharzia from the water. I forded the river on Cobber. After several more makeshift camps we eventually reached Zurak in the Wase Emirate. A private miner at Zurak who was working a small zinc mine nearby entertained us at his camp and gave us an excellent meal. When I saw the truck, the landrover and the drivers I could hardly believe that the long trek was over.

Early the next morning we piled ourselves and our essential gear, first aid box, boiled water, our lunch and Ned Kelly into the landrover. Momo, Audu, Musa Soldier and the remainder of the baggage travelled in the truck. The loads we had to leave behind at Nahuta had not yet caught up with us. As we were driving along Tony saw a small antelope and got out of the car to shoot it. In the excitement our driver forgot that we had a faulty battery and stopped the engine. We could not get it started again. There we were in the searing heat miles from nowhere. The driver had to walk back along the track to find some helpers to push our vehicle to start it. After that Tony took over the driving. Blazing along the track we saw a roan antelope and some smaller game but we could not delay as we were now behind schedule and we had to try to reach base camp before dark.

The track was getting worse and we had to slow down. I was hot, tired and half asleep when I suddenly felt as if I had been hit by an anti-tank shell and when I looked down there was blood pouring from my nose and all over my blouse and skirt. My sun glasses were smashed and a piece of the frame was embedded in my nose. I had evidently been hit by a small dry branch falling from a tree and had taken the impact in the face. Tony dragged out the first aid box and after swallowing a stiff brandy I proceeded to take stock of the damage. I washed my face in antiseptic and by this time I looked scarcely human. Fortunately I could still see and my nose was not broken, but I had a cut down it and a great piece of skin off my forehead, a cut in my cheek and two of the blackest eyes I had ever seen. All our spare clothes were in the truck so there was no way of my getting even a clean blouse and I eventually arrived at base camp looking more dead than alive. As there were quite a number of people at the camp, geologists, prospectors, labourers etc. they must have wondered what on earth had arrived when I staggered out of the landrover.

Fulani visitors to one of our temporary camps.

Chapter 8

Base Camp at Gwiwan Kogi

The Chief geologist, John Farrington, was preparing to return to the Plateau and he wanted to take me to Jos Hospital, but I said there was nothing time would not cure and I felt that I could not face another long car journey over rough bush roads. Although Ola Williams was the first white woman I had seen for months we had just a short chat and a cup of tea. I then went over to our own mud hut and went to bed.

I awoke next morning to find that I had a face like a surrealist nightmare. The African labourers were very intrigued by my appearance, and I learned later from our headman that they had decided that the master, Tony had been beating me up!!

After two or three days I felt a little better, and although I still looked terrible I went for a walk around the camp. There were four or five permanent camps for various staff members. The houses were built of mud, referred to as a pise or adobe in some countries but just plain mud in these parts. The roofs were heavily thatched and covered with zana mats to keep the building cooler. Our house consisted of several mud huts, serving as lounge, dining-room, bedroom with an adjoining bathroom. The kitchen and the storeroom were detached from the main building. All the buildings were enclosed within a zana mat fence and Audu and Momo had their houses outside the fence. All other staff members had similar houses, but Ola and Frank Williams had the luxury of a kerosene refrigerator. This was absolute joy, as for the first time in many months we were able to have a really cold drink, and meat could be kept and not have to be eaten soon after being killed. This was just as well as there were a good deal of game in this part of the country.

Of course, and rightly so, elephants and giraffes were protected and all the cat family, lions, leopards, cheetahs and other big cats were the

41

property of Sarkin Wase. I informed Ned Kelly of this but he seemed singularly unimpressed.

Most of the geologists and prospectors were ardent big game hunters and every evening after work hunting parties were organized. Many of the African workers joined the parties. I did not go as I hated game shooting although I realized it had to be done to provide meat for the workers, domestic staff and ourselves. While the hunting expeditions were on Ola and I would go for our evening walk. The weather was getting hotter and hotter and our mud houses were like ovens.

We had put our stretchers outside so that we could get some respite at night but the heat was beginning to tell on all concerned. The men were working very hard to get the prospecting and mining finished before the rains. Ola and I spent a good deal of time checking and copying geological reports to save Frank and Tony time.

During March we had a pleasant surprise with the arrival of another woman at the camp. Hannah Kennerley had just arrived from England to join her prospector husband, Juba. Hannah was very good company and during the previous dry season had accompanied her husband on an expedition to the Southern Cameroons. She stayed with us for only a short time but she and Juba kept us entertained with an account of their hilarious experiences on that rather unfortunate expedition.

Although my face still looked a terrible mess the pain had passed and I soon got to know all the people, European and African. While living at the base camp had its advantages there were certain disadvantages. We had to live in close proximity to each other, plus the fact that we had all been out in the bush for many months and also the fact that the weather was now getting unbearably hot sometimes led to minor irritations and tempers occasionally flared, but considering the diversity of age, temperament and nationality we got along amazingly well together.

The same thing could not be said for our domestic staff. Our bush cook Momo and the steward Audu were conducting a terrible brawl over the cook's young and attractive wife, Ladi. This eternal triangle dispute gave us a lot of trouble. Momo did not want to go to Wase to collect stores as he did not want to leave his wife with Audu. She would not go with him as she did not want to leave Audu. When the three of them were in camp together a non-stop fight went on. The only solution we could think of was to send all three of them to collect their own corn and market supplies. This meant that very little work was done around the camp and things became very unpleasant for all concerned.

A diversion was caused when we heard that on his next visit John

Farrington would be bringing down some mining and geological experts to inspect the prospect. We had been hearing about this proposed visit for some time and as the rainy season appeared imminent we began to wonder if it was likely to eventuate. Everyone's stores and supplies were becoming perilously low and in my case my wardrobe had reached the end of the road. My skirt had never looked too good after it was bloodstained in the accident and a rent in the back of it had to be reinforced with a piece of old pillow slip. Hannah and Ola were in a better situation as they had not been on trek, so could bring more personal effects with them. However, as they were much bigger women than I was, borrowing from them was out of the question. It looked as if my old jungle pants and my last blouse were going to be the mainstay of my wardrobe for our social occasions.

We were delighted when John Farrington, the visitors and the stores eventually arrived. The whole camp was now thrown into a flurry of entertaining. It was a pleasant change after the monotonous routine of the last few weeks. We took it in turns to entertain the guests. We managed our own particular party under fairly difficult circumstances. The eternal triangle set-up in the kitchen led to endless trouble, but with the help of Hannah's steward we managed. I had already threatened Momo and Audu that there was to be no public brawling so they conducted their ongoing fight well away from our compound. Things went smoothly and we all had a very enjoyable evening. We did receive something of a surprise when John Farrington introduced the guests, Dr Jacobsen was the director of the Government Geological Survey in Nigeria and I had known him well in my student days at Melbourne University. I knew that he was somewhere in Nigeria but he certainly received a shock when he saw me.

When I met Mr Knight I knew I had seen him somewhere before, and during the evening when he mentioned Mt. Isa I realized that he had been working as an exploration geologist with the Zinc Corporation when we were with Mt. Isa Mines. The mention of Mt. Isa started Juba Kennerley off on his tales of when he slept in the dry bed of the Leichardt River and used his boots as a pillow so that no one would steal them while he slept.

Juba was a wonderful story teller and he had worked all over the world. Although most of the camp refused to believe half his tales I at least knew that those regarding Mt. Isa were basically true. He had been there in the very early days of the mine and conditions must have been more than primitive. Sleeping in the river bed would have been easy for most of the year and if you wished to keep your boots it would have been unwise to take them off your feet and leave them around while you slept. You could get an unpleasant surprise while sleeping in the river bed. In the rainy season it could be quite dry in Mount Isa, but a sudden storm up in the hills could send water several feet deep rushing down the dry river bed. Many of the early prospectors and miners had to retreat very hurriedly from their sleeping quarters. People unused to tropical storms were often very surprised at the rapid rise and fall of the Leichardt River. I remember one morning when we were there I went over from the mine side to the town side to do some shopping. The river was quite dry when I crossed over the bridge. After I had finished my shopping and had visited a friend the river was flowing through the town where not a drop of rain had fallen. I was more than amazed but then I realized that it must have deluged in an area many miles away and it had taken some time for the flood waters to reach Mt Isa. Probably some of the visitors did not believe this story either.

The third guest, Mr Sprague, was unknown to us, but had recently done a good deal of geological work with the brother of one of our best friends, Dr Browne. By the time the party was over we felt that we were among old friends. It seemed to us that the mining world was a small world and at any gathering of mining personnel you were sure to meet someone who had worked with someone you had previously known. There were times when I felt that half the mining world must at some time have worked at Mt. Isa Mines.

It was also a great relief to me to have (at least for a while) a few topics of conversation other than big game hunting or mining. However, the respite was brief. The visitors inspected the mine site and did the geological work during the day, and in the evening John Farrington, Frank Williams and Juba Kennerley took them out hunting. These expeditions provided meat for the camp, Africans and Europeans, and most of the conversations for the evening gatherings. No matter how hard we tried to direct the conversation into other channels we always seemed to get back to hunting or mining. Sometimes I felt that given a gun I could have shot the hunters.

One of the trophies of the hunt was a greater bustard. John thought that this would be a special treat for his dinner party so when the bird was plucked and cleaned he brought it over to see if I could do something with it. I rather gathered that Ola, Hannab and their cooks would have nothing to do with it. I was still having trouble with the eternal triangle. Momo had practically given up all work except breadmaking. I was left to wrestle with the bustard. I realized that short of a pressure cooker which I did not have the bird would be scarcely edible. Steaming followed by a roasting and basting produced something tough and tasteless. I decided that a sauce made with good French wine might help, but by this time I was prepared to substitute 'bastard' for 'bustard'!

I suggested to John that it might be a good idea to ply his guests with plenty of liquor before they attacked, and that was definitely the word, the main course. The idea worked and I don't think that anyone apart from myself thought that the meat was any tougher than usual although I did notice that Clem Knight was having trouble wrestling with the poultry. As he was sitting next to me I finally whispered, 'Put your foot on it.' This was our final dinner party.

We now had definite evidence that the rainy season was fast approaching. Peter Lancaster-Jones and Hank Cole had been washed out of their camp and along with their two kittens had moved into base camp.

When John Farrington and the visiting geologists were ready to return to the Plateau we were told that our bush tour was officially over, and with the impending wet season it would be advisable for us to pack up and prepare to return to the mine headquarters at Rayfield. This had to be done in fairly easy stages as there was a large amount of gear, and only a limited number of motor vehicles in which to transport it. For various reasons it was decided that Ola and I would be the first to leave. Tom John also had to get away as he was booked for leave to the United Kingdom and had to return to the Plateau to complete maps and reports prior to his departure.

Ola and I travelled in the landrover. Even with an early morning start the day was hot and uncomfortable, and a very long journey over a rough and dusty road was not an inviting prospect. However, once we started the ascent to the Plateau it became much more bearable. We stopped at the Pankshin rest house for lunch. This was a delightful rest house very different from some of the 'pest houses' we had occupied during the early part of our trek. It had a magnificent position, on the edge of an escarpment overlooking the broad Wase River valley, and surrounded by a beautiful garden.

There were dozens of frangipanni trees covered in masses of blossoms, cream, pink, white, apricot and red, jacaranda trees in full bloom, as well as poincianas, bouganvilleas, pride of Barbados and Bird of Paradise flowers.

Later we passed through a belt of palm trees, but as we climbed higher, the vegetation changed and by the time we reached Dorowa we were back with the typical Plateau scenery. We finally reached Bukuru at dusk. Here we discovered that there had been a last minute change of arrangements. We were not expected and no one knew where we were going to stay.

Finally we were taken to Rayfield Guest House, an establishment usually reserved for V.I.P. visitors, but we had to live somewhere. Ola looked tired and worn out but the sight of a full length bath and a decent mattress revived my spirits considerably. After feeding Ned Kelly I just fell into bed and, thanks to the coolness and comfort, overslept.

By the end of April the entire party was back on the Plateau. Last to arrive was Peter Lancaster-Jones and his cat Little John, now more appropriately called Little Joanna.

The return of the expedition marked many changes. Frank Williams took charge of the Geological Department at Rayfield and Tony and Tom John elected to stay with the company, and work on tin and columbite with Frank until they were ready to go on leave. On their return they were to form part of a mining and geological team working on the Tunga prospect in the Wase area. Juba Kennerley went to work in the Southern Areas of our mining company while Bob Hurley decided to leave our company, A.T.M.N., and join another company based on the Plateau. 'Pat' Lewis left Nigeria to work in what was at that time Southern Rhodesia, while Lancaster-Jones returned to England and later joined the Cementation Company and the Cementation Ground Engineering Ltd. as an engineering geologist. He had a long and distinguished career with these companies.

Hank Cole went to what was formerly known as British Guyana and we never heard from him again.

Sadly we also lost Ned Kelly. As we were preparing to go on leave we had to find a home for Ned. I did not know anyone on the Plateau well enough to leave Ned in their care but as our good friends Ruth and Walter Erbele were at their mission headquarters they decided to take Ned. We knew that he would have a good home at their mission in the bush but unfortunately when they were packing up to return to their station Ned escaped and in spite of an intensive search was never found. We were very sad at the loss of our little companion who had given us many happy hours when we were on trek.

About this time I was introduced to two other geologists working for A.T.M.N., Karol Paulo and Robin Watson. They had not been part of our expedition but were working on a prospect in Southern Nigeria. Our next two months were spent living in a transit house at Yelwa Club finalising our preparations for leave. Tony was in desperate need of a change. He had served two arduous bush tours and had worked for nearly two years instead of the usual eighteen months tour. I was looking forward to seeing new countries and people.

Chapter 9

The Second Bush Tour

When we were in London we often discussed arrangements for our next tour in the bush. We knew that in many ways it would be entirely different from previous tours. These had been primarily of a geological and prospecting nature and the work had been done mainly by geologists and prospectors. Now that the most favourable site, a prospect at Tunga in the Wase area, had been selected for mining much of the work would now have to be done by miners and drillers under the supervision of a mining engineer. As a result the geological staff had been reduced to two and five drillers and a mining engineer had been added to the team. I had been introduced to the mining engineer, George Connor while I was in London but the remainder of the team, four from the United Kingdom and one from Canada were strangers to me.

The company had suggested that the two geologists, Tony and Tom John, should make an early start by selecting a suitable spot for a base camp as well as preparing sites for the drillers to commence drilling. Tony left London towards the end of September and commenced work as soon as possible. As the rains were not then properly over a good deal of the work had to be carried out under difficult and unpleasant conditions. Much of the area was still under water and the roads and tracks were either quagmires or non-existent and the heavy drilling equipment could not be located on site. Until a permanent camp was built I could not join the expedition so I remained in England for a little longer and then returned to Nigeria on a Dutch cargo ship which called at some African parts that I had not previously seen including Dakar and Monrovia.

As the mud hut at Gwiwan Kogi had proved so unsatisfactory during the previous tour it was decided to make the base camp huts of zana mats. This could not be done until the rains were over, as while the zana mat huts were definitely cooler they were certainly not waterproof. In the meantime the men lived in tents.

I was ready to leave the Plateau by mid November and this time I made the long and uncomfortable journey in an old truck over a rough, dusty road. As we were able to get right into base camp without the use of head porters I was able to take along a few more comforts. While we were in London I had purchased an inflatable rubber mattress. It was not exactly inner-sprung but was a considerable improvement on the piece of corrugated kapok that I had used as a mattress on the earlier tour. I was also able to take a few more clothes and personal possessions including a portable gramophone and records.

Our first stop was at Wase. Long before we reached Wase we could see Wase Rock. This trachyte plug, about nine hundred feet in height, stood in the middle of a plain and dominated the country for miles around. It was steep on all sides and was reputed to be unscalable. According to report in previous years condemned prisoners were offered the choice of execution or climbing the rock. As far as was known no one ever succeeded in climbing it. Apart from the sheer sides of the rock, climbing trachyte rocks is always a dangerous exercise. Even with good climbing gear the brittle nature of the rock is always a hazard. About thirty miles from our present home in Queensland there are several of these trachyte plugs known as the Glasshouse Mountains. Although they are popular with rock climbers there have been many nasty accidents due to the brittle nature of the rock.

When we reached Wase I called on the Emir. I was invited up to his palace, a very large mud edifice. I signed the visitors' book and he took me to see his cats. The poor things were in cages that were far too small and I was very thankful that he did not have any leopards in the collection. The bush cats had obviously been teased a great deal by the palace retainers and some of them looked very strange. I could not blame the poor beasts.

I did not leave the Emir the customary dash as I did not know whether it might be an infringement of palace etiquette. Later when I got to know him better I found that he loved magazines, particularly the Australian *Women's Weekly*. These were sent to me by friends and relatives and were in the category of ancient history by the time I received them, but he always enjoyed receiving a bundle of them when he visited our camp. He said that he enjoyed the coloured pictures.

When we reached Tunga Prospect I met the new members of our expedition staff, George Connor the Australian mining engineer and the five

Myself, Momo, Sarkin Wase, George Connor and Hassan at Tunga Prospect.

drillers. I had already met George in London. At the same time I was introduced to our new bush cook. After all the nonsense which we had endured with Ladi, Momo and Audu on our previous tour I had asked Tony to engage a new cook and steward.

The new cook, another Momo, was one of the most delightful persons that I had ever met. He was to remain with us for the next eighteen years. He was always cheerful, had a pleasant personality and the ability to get on with everyone, Europeans and Africans. He could also bake excellent bread and as I could cook almost everything else we managed very well.

The camp at Tunga Prospect was adequate, and our greatest boon was the kerosene refrigerator. However, when Sarkin Wase visited us he was not very impressed and said that he had not expected to see a European woman living in such a fashion and he kindly made me a dash of some mats to keep the dust down. Sarkin Wase was a young man. He had visited the United Kingdom and was anxious that the mining venture should prove successful as he wanted more work and prosperity in his district. He was very helpful in recruiting additional labourers for our work force. He wanted more work for his people and co-operated in this respect with our

headman, Mallam Hassan. In one of my diaries I still have a letter he
wrote to Tony in 1952:

'With reference to your letter dated September 16th 1952 I have to
inform you that all your accounts were quite understood. We found
Mallam Hassan is a kind fellow and immediately he arrived many labourers went to him so far as they know his manner. All of these were done by
the time I was at Kaduna. Thanking you for your kindness.
Compliments.

Sincerely yours,
Abdullah Kano.
Sarkin Wase.

Now that the dry season had set in and the drilling and geological work
were going smoothly we once again began to think of Christmas. Our
Christmas celebrations at Tunga turned out very differently from the
lonely Christmas Tony and I and Bob Hurley had spent at Diji the previous year.

Oliver Hunt, the District Officer in the Shendam Division, kindly invited all Europeans in the area to celebrate Christmas with him. We were
rather a mixed lot of guests, as apart from the seven of us from the Tunga
Prospect there were a number of administrative officers from outlying
stations as well as a couple of Catholic priests from their mission stations.
As part of the celebrations Oliver Hunt decided to hold a race meeting.

The Africans loved race meetings and Oliver Hunt, John Wilson and
Tom Hollington-Sawyer were all excellent horsemen. Several others, not
quite so good, also took part. We also ran a tote for betting on the various
events. The race meeting was not exactly a fashion parade, any resem-
blance to Ascot or the Melbourne Cup being quite accidental. There were
only two European women present. The wife of one of the administration
officers had recently come out from England to be with her husband over
Christmas. She looked quite attractive in a fashionable frock, while I wore
a dreadful much washed cotton dress topped with a straw hat purchased in
the Wase market. The hat was trimmed with a beautiful scarf sent by a
relative as a Christmas present. However, the fashion honours went to a
young Pagan girl whose entire costume consisted of a pink brassiere and
bunches of leaves worn fore and aft. Where she had obtained the brassiere
remained a mystery, but African women were always keen to wear foundation garments.

The practice was not confined to women. Years later when I was living on the Plateau I remember Natalie Cooke telling me that she had thrown out some old fashioned pink laced corsets worn by her mother (the legendary Kitty). She never knew what happened to them until one day she went down to confer with her head gardener and found to her amazement that he was wearing Kitty's old corset. Although Momo's wife and daughters always wore African dress and had little interest in any of the discarded frocks they were always keen to obtain brassieres and other foundation garments.

Once the Christmas celebrations were over we all returned to our daily routine. Tony decided to leave the Tunga Prospect and conduct his exploration work from the pagan village of Mageria. Apart from being nearer to his work we realized that with another five months ahead in the hottest time of the year tensions were likely to arise in such a close knit community virtually living in each other's pockets. One of the drillers had already returned to England, and George Connor, the Australian mining engineer, was not exactly enamoured of another five months in the bush. George had thought that his work would have finished in eight weeks, not eight months, and with a wife and young child in Australia, life in the African bush was far from satisfying. By January 3rd we were ready for our move. Early in the morning our headman, and some labourers set out with our effects. As there was as yet no road for the landrover they had to trek. My last job was to clean out the refrigerator. I hated leaving it but realized that there were more people at the prospect and their need was greater than ours.

In the afternoon Umoru came over with the landrover and Tony and I with our personal belongings clambered on board while Musa Kano making his second trip came with us. Not long after leaving Mageria we got into an absolute sea of elephant grass about ten feet high. We could not see the ground ahead of us and Tony was afraid of wrecking the landrover on hidden stumps and holes. Musa got on top of the loads in the back of the landrover and from that precarious position endeavoured to spy out ant beds, logs and other hazards in our path. All I hoped was that there were no pits, animal traps or rocks underneath as we could see absolutely nothing. To make matters worse it was burning off time and fires and smoke made driving conditions even more hazardous. Finally things became so bad that the landrover had to be abandoned. A guard was placed over our stores and we carried as much as we could and finished the journey on foot. We finally reached the village. It looked like dozens of other villages we had passed through but with the difference that this was to be our 'home' for the next four or five months.

Our appearance scarcely qualified us for the reception which we received. It was only later that I discovered that I was the chief cause for the celebration. As was the case with Diji on the earlier tour the villagers had only very occasionally seen a white man. Tony had earlier visited the spot to select a site for our camp, and at very remote intervals a government official passed through the village. A white woman was a creature the villagers had never set eyes on before. Covered with dust at that moment I scarcely qualified for the title, but curiosity was rampant. The result was predictable. The children reacted most violently, the majority let out terrified yells and dashed behind mother's skirts or where mother's skirts could have been if she had such an item of clothing. When the pandemonium calmed down a little the village chief, a particularly repulsive looking individual, welcomed us and led us up to the site of our future home.

Chapter 10

The House at Mageria

The house was situated in rather a pleasant spot under two shady trees. It was made of zana mats and was rather similar to the camp we had at Diji, but this one even had doors. Zana mats were rather too heavy to use as doors so these were made of corn stalks. These stalks were similar to bamboo canes. The mats given to us by Sarkin Wase were placed on the floor of the 'lounge-dining room' A high zana mat fence was built around the house as, apart from giving us a certain amount of privacy, we knew that as the weather became hotter we should have to move the beds outside and sleep out there. Actually it became so unbearably hot during March and April we virtually lived in the enclosure as the evening meal was also taken out of doors.

We soon settled into our new camp. As usual Tony selected a site for a well and well sinking commenced at once. Once again I started a garden. I planted beans, radishes and tomatoes.

It was not long before we got to know our neighbours. The pagans of Mageria village belong to a division of the Yergum tribe and the chief occupations were farming and hunting. In common with practically all pagan tribes of Northern Nigeria they had tribal marks on their faces. The tribal marks of the Yergum were of three types. The first consisted of three pairs of two inch long lines radiating from the outer corner of each eye, the second type a stripe on each side of the face from the temple to above the chin and thirdly four short horizontal lines at the corner of each eye. Most of the people of Mageria were marked in the latter fashion. This custom of tribal marking was originally adopted so that the chief could recognize his subjects at a glance, and members of one tribe could not stray to another. Although this practice of tribal marking is gradually dying out it still persists in the more remote areas.

The house at Mageria – our most comfortable bush home. Note the corn stalk door.

The various pagan tribes of Northern Nigeria had much in common, but each had its own particular customs. Many tribes had nothing to do with each other at all, although their villages might be only a short distance apart. Marriage between tribes was not common, and if allowed was restricted to certain tribes. In the case of the Yergum no woman was allowed to leave her own country. Most of the tabus were for economic reasons. The majority of the pagans were hard workers and the people of Mageria were no exception and men, women and children all worked on the farms during planting and harvesting. As previously mentioned the Yergum were keen agriculturalists and large areas were cultivated. The chief crops were the grain crops dawa and gero, but quantities of ground nuts (peanuts), beans, cassava, cotton and tobacco were also grown. Owing to the large area under corn we found that the village was quite extensive. There was normally a small group of mud huts, corn bins, etc, then an acre or so of grain crops, then more houses. The chief and his entourage occupied the most important buildings in the centre of the village.

Our arrival occurred during harvest time and each day I used to see entire families at work. Even the youngest children helped. They picked the lower heads of grain and carried small bundles home on their heads. Dawa or Guinea corn grew to a considerable height, and just before it

The author outside the house at Mageria.

ripened, the villagers would go through the corn, with long forked sticks with which they bent over each stalk three or four feet from the top. This served to plump the grain and brought it within easy reach of their curved harvesting knives. The older women carried large bundles of corn cobs on their heads with the greatest unconcern and I remember one day seeing a woman walking along with a baby strapped on her back, a toddler astride one hip and a huge bundle of corn on her head. Added to this she was in an advanced stage of pregnancy.

The villagers soon got to know us and became very friendly. I had many visitors, particularly from the young people. One morning two girls called as I was fixing up a bunch of flowers I had collected from the bush. I took a couple of the flowers and tucked flowers behind their ears in the South Sea island fashion. They giggled and went away, but three or four days later several girls arrived all with leaves or flowers tucked in their hair. Maybe I had started a new fashion.

Clothing and dress were no great problem. In common with most other pagan tribes the Yergum wore the minimum of clothing. Children of both sexes went around naked while the women wore small bunches of green leaves in front and behind. The men wore a leather belt around their hips.

I believe that many of the tribes of Northern Nigeria were called pagan because of the fact that they went around naked or almost so. It had nothing to do with their religious practices or lack of them. One soon became used to this near nudity and after a few days took no notice of it. In fact when I returned to Jos on the Plateau I was rather surprised to see some of the pagan women wearing a kind of a sari garment of unbleached cloth with the usual bunch of leaves poking through the back. However, this was worn only when they came into the town and those working in the fields near our home soon discarded it.

About this time we ran into a little trouble with social practices in the district. Game was fairly plentiful in the area and one day Tony shot a roan antelope. These were large animals and a good deal of the meat was left at the Tunga camp. After distribution to the African and European personnel there he brought the remainder back to Mageria. It was given to Momo our bush cook for distribution, but we later discovered that he kept most of it for himself, the headman and immediate friends. When a second antelope was shot Tony decided on a more equitable distribution by dividing it into equal portions for each man regardless of social status. However, he had reckoned without Nigerian ideas and next day there were repercussions. Momo and Musa took exception to being bracketed with the horse boy and the wood and water boy so decided to accept no meat.

They compelled young Ali Bashar and one or two others to accept this very hard decision.

The local chief arrived in much greater umbrage and announced that as he had not been sent a leg the price of corn to our staff and labourers would be increased from fourpence to one shilling per mudu. His was a telling method of attack as we were many miles from the nearest corn market at Wase and the labour forces were heavily dependent on the village for corn.

Tony held the ace, however, and said that if there was going to be all the fuss he would not shoot any more game for meat. Finally everything was settled amicably and in future the meat was to be given to Musa the headman and he was to distribute it. He always kept the best portions for himself and his friends.

On one occasion Tony asked for the head to be returned as he wished to keep it for a trophy. Momo buried it for cleaning purposes and I promptly forgot all about it until a week or so later I saw a small group of children gathered around the burial spot and I decided to investigate. A party was in progress. The children had dug up the head and were eating with great relish the meat adhering to it. It was more than high, but they seemed to be enjoying it, as much as many children would enjoy sweets such as ice cream. No article of food was considered too repulsive for pagan stomachs.

In earlier days it was a common practice for certain tribes, particularly the Jarawa, to eat corpses of their tribe, particularly those of thieves or other criminals. Some tribes being a bit more squeamish than others would exchange corpses with other tribes. This abominable custom had been more or less stamped out in villages closer to civilization. Whether cannibalism was practised in Mageria I could not say. Such customs would naturally be kept well hidden from us.

After the harvest had been gathered in, the villagers had much more spare time and social life became much more evident. Night after night we heard drum beating and singing. At these functions large quantities of home made beer brewed from the local corn was drunk. Though not habitual drunkards the Yergum did consume excessive quantities of home made beer on festive occasions. After harvest celebrations would last all night and in the morning one could sometimes witness the sorry spectacle of the entire population of the village, excluding the youngest children suffering from a gigantic hangover. I always found it rather strange that one of the crimes levelled at the white race in connection with coloured people was that they brought the vice of alcoholism to them. This was

hardly fair as in many primitive societies I have known these people have
made their own potent beverages.

Chapter 11

Dodos and Jujus

It was at the end of the harvest that I had my first meeting with a ghost. Most people who have had encounters with ghosts have recollections of clanking chains, dim rooms in turreted castles, and ethereal figures floating past, sometimes with their heads and sometimes without. My encounter with the ghostly world was somewhat different. It took place on a very hot dusty afternoon on a bush track just outside Mageria village. Every afternoon it was my custom to go for a walk. The scenery was not very exciting, and all I usually saw were a few pagan women working in their gardens or tending yam plots. Sometimes I would see a small animal such as a ground squirrel and I always kept a wary eye out for snakes which were all too prevalent in this district. However I certainly did not expect to see what I could only describe as an animated haystack. There were several corn stacks along the path but this one was rather different as it was definitely moving. I stood rooted to the spot for a few seconds and then did a fast about turn and hastened back to our camp still being followed by the corn stack apparition. Tony was still out working so to make sure that I had not been seeing things or suffering from hallucinations I called out to my friend and helper Momo, and asked him if he had an explanation. He just gave me a withering look and told me that I had seen a dodo or pagan ghost. Momo had little respect for pagan customs but I was determined to find out more about dodos.

Dodos were mythical spirits well known in West Africa. The most common type seen were the maskers, and they were sometimes seen at Mageria during the dry season. They were supposed to represent the ghosts of the deceased, and were dressed in elaborate costumes which entirely covered them. Many of the costumes were made of straw and this was the type that I had encountered. Other costumes were made from woven material with anklets and bracelets of cowrie shells. At one time in Nigeria cowrie shells were used as currency so were readily available. Once in the area of the Angas pagans I saw a dodo in a costume which looked as if it had been knitted, but probably was some intricate type of weaving. The face was always masked so that the women and children had no idea of the identity of the dodo.

These dodos sometimes exercised a disciplinary influence over the women by allotting punishment to those who had given their husbands

Types of dodos. The 'animated haystack type' mentioned in the story is on the far right.

trouble, but their most important function was to dance at funerals. However, custom demanded the postponement of their celebrations until after the harvest so that they often coincided with other festivals and the dodos were seen in the interval between harvest and sowing. There was no doubt that the chief of Mageria village adapted the dodo to suit his own ends.

When we first arrived at the village I had wondered why our house had not been built under a big tree, a short distance from the site chosen, but Tony told me that he had wanted to have it built there but the chief had opposed the suggestion as it was the juju tree area and the local dodo visited there. The chief kept a certain amount of law and order in the village by means of these dodo men and they were a powerful weapon to the men in the tribe for keeping the women in subjection. The meetings were held in a patch of dense scrub surrounding the tree. When a dodo meeting was to be held the women were given ample warning, as their first duty was to appease his wrath. Chickens and goats were prepared and beer provided. The women were then told to go and hide. Generally only married men were admitted to dodo societies. When a new group of young initiates were to be admitted to the society an extra large feast was prepared.

The young men about to be admitted were given a severe flogging as part of the tribal acceptance. This served a dual purpose as the shrieks of the new members helped the women to believe that some infernal spirit was loose in the bushes, while the victims were terrorized into announcing that they would never reveal the identity of the dodo even under pain of death.

After this ordeal a general feasting of the dodo's food followed. The meeting broke up in pandemonium with much shrieking and yelling. Finally a fearful noise was made by one of the men blowing through a calabash. This eerie noise was more or less an all clear signal to let the women know that the dodo had departed.

Ordinary meetings were often a method of dealing with those who had infringed the tribal laws, and I am quite convinced that on some occasions the accused was put to death and buried on the spot. The rest of the crowd then danced over the area and all trace of the crime obliterated. If anyone was foolish enough to comment on the disappearance there was always the simple explanation that the dodo had eaten him.

Everyone treated the juju area with a certain amount of respect. Most of the women were terrified of the spot and would not go near it. Even Momo, although he laughed at the idea of the dodo never went within the precincts of the grove. At it was our custom always to interfere as little as possible with village life we also treated the juju area with a certain amount of respect and kept well away from the place. Personally I detested it, and regretted that our camp had to be placed so close to the site, but as this was the only place where there was a reasonable amount of shade we had no real alternative.

Chapter 12

The Eclipse and the Deluge

Probably the most interesting natural phenomenon that we observed while in this area was a total eclipse of the sun. This occurred on February 25th. The best place in the world to observe this eclipse was the Sudan. Expeditions were sent from places around the world: Britain, Canada, the United States, Italy, Eire, France, Holland, Egypt, Greece and Switzerland all set up observation posts across the continent from French Equatorial Africa to as far away as Saudi Arabia.

We obtained a splendid view of the eclipse. I was anxious to observe the villagers' reaction to it and discovered that they took no notice of it at all. We had told Momo what would happen but he dismissed it with his usual phrase, regarding anything about the weather, 'If Allah wills it.'

The eclipse gave us a very welcome, if temporary respite from the blazing African sun. The temperature dropped 15° Fahrenheit while the eclipse lasted. Whether it was a contributing factor I do not know but some hours after the eclipse we received two inches of rain in two hours, an unprecedented occurrence in the middle of the dry season. Our zana mat hut was fairly cool and comfortable but definitely not waterproof. When the rain started Tony placed a tarpaulin over the frames of our mosquito nets. It was a very makeshift protection and soon filled with muddy water as the zana mat roof was full of dust. The weight of water soon broke the mosquito net frames and dumped all the muddy water over the beds. The mosquito nets, stretchers, bed linen to say nothing of ourselves were absolutely saturated. As everything was so wet and filthy we decided that we would move outside where we would be no wetter but somewhat cleaner. Fortunately Tony always kept his maps, films and other records, cameras and my diaries in steel trunks.

One result of our unseasonable deluge was that I got to know Gabriel Ladele. We were all busy pegging out our various belongings on make-shift lines when a rather shy young African came over to ask if he could give us any help. I knew him by sight and had heard Tony say that he was by far the most intelligent compass boy that he had ever employed. As Gabriel spoke fluent English it was not long before I learnt a lot more about him. He was a Yoruba and had been educated as a Christian at a Baptist mission in the Western Region of Nigeria. Apart from speaking and writing English he could also speak Hausa and understood a certain amount of some pagan dialects. His handwriting was some of the finest that I have ever seen, and that included my father's, and he had something of a fetish about beautiful handwriting.

Tony decided that Gabriel's abilities were not being fully used as a compass boy and began to teach him the rudiments of surveying. He learnt quickly and when we returned to the plateau we had him transferred to the Survey Department where he was fully trained as a surveyor. He remained with the company for many years. After the dreadful tribal massacre he often dropped in for a chat and told me that as Yoruba and a Christian he was not too happy at living in a predominantly Hausa and Muslim country and thought that it might be advisable for him to return to his own Yoruba country in the Western Region of Nigeria. He and his wife did eventually return to Oyo where he acquired a cattle property, and did very well with the farming project. He also entered local politics but soon became disillusioned with that.

He told me that when we were living on the outskirts of the pagan village at Mageria he actually lived in the village. He said that he was quite sure that the Yergum managed to get rid of any of the tribe that did not appeal to them, and that much of the drumming and dancing, and infernal din that we heard at night often covered more sinister activities. He also said that at that time he was quite sure that the Jukuns still practised cannibalism.

Gabriel still writes to us once or twice a year and we exchange photos and Christmas cards. Sometimes I find it hard to believe that it is over forty years since we first became friends.

After we had cleaned up most of the mess from the downpour George Connor came over from Tunga to see how we had fared. They had evidently had even more rain than we received. It upset the programme as the flooded prospect trenches had left the prospect in a shambles and drilling was delayed for some time. In the thick of the deluge Roy Noel had gone over to see the Canadian driller, Len Metcalfe. Len invited him in out of the rain! As their huts were like ours I gathered that the invitation was superfluous. Tom John came over later and said that he had not received quite as much rain at his outpost.

Many years later we experienced another unseasonable deluge, but in this case there was very little, if any, scientific basis for the downpour. We were living at Crown Bird creek between Bukuru and Rayfield on the Plateau. The rainy season was very late starting that year and I had noticed the pagan tribe (once again the pagans were my nearest neighbours) were having trouble getting their crops planted. The ground was very hard to dig and the young plants had to be hand watered and were dying off. There was very little water in Crown Bird Creek and we were having a struggle to keep our garden watered. One day I saw Momo having a long talk with some local pagans. I found this rather unusual as he normally had little to do with them. I asked him if anything was wrong, and he said that the pagans had told him that there was no rain because of the bird's nest in the large fig tree in our garden.

During the previous year some hammerkops had built a nest in the tree. The birds, sometimes called anvil head or more commonly hammerkop, were so named because of the shape of their heads. The flattened bill at one end of the head and a horizontal crest of feathers at the back gave the head the appearance of an anvil. The birds were sometimes seen around our part of the world but never in large numbers. The strangest thing about them was the type of nest that they built. The nest was very large, the one in our fig tree being about three feet deep and about four and a half feet in width. It was extremely unsightly, being made up of sticks, old rags, socks or anything else that could be used for nest building. The whole thing was held together by a lining of mud or dung or both. The following year they built on to the nest and the whole thing looked like a slum tenement, and we decided that it would have to be removed. Then someone said, 'Oh, don't take it down. It is supposed to be very lucky to have hammerkops build in your garden.' I forgot about it, and the leaves of the fig tree hid a good deal of the mess. However, the dry season dragged on and the pagans kept asking Momo to get us to take the nest down so I finally said to him, 'Do you think it would rain if we got rid of the nest?' I got the inevitable answer, 'If Allah wills it.'

The next morning I was going shopping in Jos. It was a fine hot morning with a clear sky so I told Momo to inform the pagans that they could remove the nest provided that every scrap of rubbish was removed before I returned. He was to oversee the whole operation. When I returned at lunchtime the demolition job was completed, and it looked as if rain was as far away as ever – Yes, you have probably guessed it – just after four o'clock that afternoon the heavens opened! It hardly stopped raining for the next three months.

Rain making was a subject taken fairly seriously in some parts of Nigeria, and the rainmaker had not only to make it rain, but he had also to be able to control or stop it. Various methods were used to make rain, and some of the rituals were quite impressive. Sometimes water, porridge or blood was poured on the ground to placate evil spirits and to ensure that rain would fall. At other times black clothes were worn to symbolize rain clouds, and an encroaching storm. Storms at the beginning and the end of the rainy season could be quite frightening. I was used to severe storms in the Pacific Islands but people from Europe sometimes found the terrific cracks of thunder and the vivid flashes of lightning quite terrifying.

The heavy rain at Mageria was the end of the cooler weather, and after that the weather became hotter and hotter, and as the conditions became more unpleasant illness became more prevalent. The queue at my morning sick parade became longer and I began to think that even the village medicine man was off-loading some of his patients on to me. Apart from the usual sore eyes, toothache, fever, constipation, diarrhoea, etc., some seemed to be suffering from complaints that I knew nothing about and could not treat. One unfortunate man must have had a poisoned foot and the local medicine man decided to cut it off. The patient evidently objected. Fortunately we were able to get him away to a mission hospital.

Illness also troubled the European workers. Len Metcalfe had a nasty form of tinea on his feet and Tony and Tom John were looking thoroughly wretched. They had been working on a prospect near Tom's camp but had both become so ill that the work had to be suspended while they went to the mission hospital. It was discovered that they had bacillary dysentery. The trouble was traced to their drinking water. The only domestic help Tom had at his camp was a local village boy who did not understand that all drinking water was to be boiled and filtered. The bacillary dysentery proved quite serious for Tony and Tom as it was to plague them for the remainder of the bush tour.

The heat and harmattan were also taking their toll on health and tempers. The drillers visited us much more frequently, mainly I thought to get away from each other. Fortunately about this time we had visits from some overseas geologists and this was good for morale. Richard Bogue, a geologist from Tucson, Arizona paid us a short visit. It was a particularly pleasant interlude for me as he brought his wife with him. While the men were out working Kay and I had a happy time together. It was delightful to have a European woman to talk to, as apart from the visitor who spent Christmas at Shendam, Kay was the only white woman I had seen in nearly four months.

Fortunately my little garden was flourishing so we had the addition of beans, tomatoes and radishes to vary the menu. Kay was delighted as they had been working in an area of Southern Nigeria where very little fresh food had been available. The villagers, intrigued by the sight of another white woman, paid us several calls. A number of the girls decided to put on a dance for us. They had been drinking a large amount of the local home brew and appeared to be very drunk. The dances were rather lewd, and in the fine frenzy their bunches of leaves fell off so that their costumes consisted mainly of their earrings. The local chief gave us a chicken, three pawpaws and two eggs. My dash to him was a five pound bag of salt and a steamed pudding. We soon disposed of the eggs and pawpaws but the chicken promptly returned to the chief.

When Tony and Richard Bogue had to do some geological work some distance from Mageria George Connor drove Kay over from Tunga to spend the night with me. By this time there was a rough road between the two camps and it was possible to make the journey by landrover. The first time it arrived the entire population of the village turned out to see it as it was definitely the first motor vehicle most of them had seen.

I was glad of Kay's company as I did not fancy the idea of spending nights alone in this spot. We were uncomfortably close to the juju area and apart from that there were large numbers of drunken revellers around and the infernal din, drumming, singing and dog barking going on during the night made sleep impossible. Strange to say, while Kay was with me things were very quiet. About this time one of the labourers gave me a baby duiker, a very small deer. It was the prettiest little thing and I named him Freddie. Bambi would probably have been more appropriate but I thought it was a bit hackneyed. Sadly I did not have Freddie for long. We did not have any fresh milk and he just did not thrive on Horlicks or tinned milk.

Tony and Richard Bogue eventually returned from their expedition. The whole party looked incredibly filthy. Africans and Europeans being covered in dust looked much the same shade, the whites looking darker and the blacks whiter under their stain. After a clean up and some photo taking the Bogues piled into the landrover and went back to Tunga from where they were to go on to Zurack. I was sorry to see them go as their visit had been a pleasant break at a particularly trying time. We kept in touch with each other for some time after their return to Arizona.

After the Bogues left we began to get intermittent showers of rain so Tony decided that we would soon have to think of moving back to the Tunga Prospect. We could manage to get stores, mail etc. over the rough bush track while the weather remained dry, but once there was any heavy rain we were definitely cut off as such a track would be quite impossible for any motor vehicle. Tom John in his even more remote prospect was in an even worse situation. When Tony was over at Tom's prospect discussing the intended move I decided to check stores and make lists of the first things that would have to go back to Tunga.

One day while I was writing lists I heard a terrific commotion at our well. This was sited near the juju area and had proved of great benefit to the village. It was a great meeting place for the village girls who combined water carrying with local gossip. They often called in to see me on the way to and from the well and they always enjoyed the spectacle of me washing and drying my hair.

It appeared that there was a move towards female emancipation in Mageria village. While some of the lasses were getting water from the well, one girl braver or perhaps more foolish than the rest decided to take a peep through the bushes in the juju area, and then told the girls that there was really no man in there at all and the juju was just a stick with grass on it. The girls were very excited, but I expected repercussions from the village chief and the local elders!

Tony arrived back in the evening. He had shot an antelope and a couple of bush fowl. We kept the bush fowl for our own use as they made a pleasant variation to our diet. Gabriel, the domestic staff and some of the labourers shared the antelope. They said that while they were out in the bush that they had seen four giraffes, three fully grown ones and a baby. Of course these beautiful animals were protected. While we were in the bush most of the men saw giraffes in their wild state, but I was never fortunate enough to do so. However, one morning I did see a beautiful sight, about forty large birds flew overhead in a mass migration. They looked like an enlarged Peter Scott painting, and were probably making for the Benue River.

I soon discovered that there were definite repercussions following the incident at the well and the encroachment on the juju area. Gabriel told me that the village elders had warned the girl who had broken the tabu that if she continued to draw water from the well she would die. Gabriel thought that they might well be right, but did not think that the cause of the death would be entirely natural. She did continue to draw water, and seemed to have given the elders the local equivalent of 'phooey to all that'. I did not think that the juju would ever be such a potent force again. In fact I did not think that it would be very long before the whole thing was laughed out of existence.

About this time the pagans were once again burning off so that with the onset of the rains fresh green grass would be available for the stock. Some of the raging fires were quite awe-inspiring, but they always seemed to be kept under control, and after my experience at Diji I realized that they did not impose the threat that always accompanied bush fires in Australia. The combination of dust and smoke from the burning off made our living conditions very unpleasant. The dust gave me a good deal of eye trouble and as Tony and Tom John were still suffering from the effects of bacillary dysentery we were anxious to get back to Tunga so that, if necessary, the two men could get to the mission hospital at Langtang.

Chapter 13

Return to Camp at Tunga Prospect

Our departure did not create the same excitement as our arrival. Some of the young girls and children came to see me off and I distributed small farewell gifts. Musa Kano and I set off in the landrover, by now a familiar sight in the area. I took our personal effects plus most of our perishable stores. Tony remained behind to supervise the distribution of head loads for the trek, look after the labourers and take his leave of the village chief. I had no doubt that our zana mat house would soon be dismantled. I often wondered whether the juju area was declared off-limits to the girls, but I think they had probably become emancipated enough to realize the advantages of being able to get water from the well which Tony had sited.

I found it strange to be back at Tunga again with so many people around but Momo was overjoyed. He was always very social with the labourers and he loved going to Wase on market day. We soon got the place in order again and by the time Tony, Tom John and Gabriel arrived we were well established. Our main consideration was the weather. By the end of April we were getting intermittent thunderstorms which indicated that the rainy season was not far off, and we were all worrying how we would get out of the area if the wet season really set in as bridges would be washed away and the road from Wase to Pankshin would be almost impassable. When the messenger came down from the plateau with our stores we learned that there had been some discussion as to whether the geological and mining team would be left out in the bush for the rainy season!!! There was a great shortage of housing for company personnel on the mines field, and someone with very little or no knowledge of bush conditions in the Gombe area thought that leaving us out for the rainy season would help solve the problem.

A government official who lived in an established house in the Shendam division said that it would be very unwise; personally I thought the idea plain crazy – stark staring mad would have been a more accurate description, as living in tents and grass houses would have been quite impossible as most of the prospecting area would have been under water. Added to this there would have been no hope of getting any stores and if anyone took dangerously ill the whole situation would have been very serious.

The suggestion that we could spend the wet season in the bush was received with considerable consternation at the camp. I said that no matter who was going to be left in the bush I was returning to the Plateau and if no accommodation could be found I would be returning to Holland on the *Nigerstroom* which was scheduled to sail from Lagos in mid-June. I knew at this time that I had a medical condition which would require surgery and a sojourn of months in an extremely isolated and unhealthy area was quite out of the question. George Connor the mining engineer said that he was going back to Australia no matter what, and as the drillers could not possibly work in the wet conditions they and their heavy equipment had to be got out as soon as possible. Fortunately when the proposal was put to the General Manager of A.T.M.N. he dismissed the whole idea as ridiculous, and said that the whole expedition was to return to the Plateau where temporary accommodation would be found in the transit houses and guest houses until the whole matter was sorted out. However, as nothing could be done for some time it looked as if we would be at Tunga Camp until the end of May.

The weather was growing hotter and hotter and we were all becoming very cranky, as the long tour was beginning to tell on everyone's nerves.

Fortunately two things brightened us up a lot. As the young Cornish driller, Roy Noel, was going to celebrate his 21st birthday at the camp I decided to have a birthday party to cheer everyone up. I remembered that my own 21st birthday had been spent at a very isolated spot in Australia miles from my family so I decided something better would have to be done for Roy. The first thing I had to get was a cake. As I had neither the ingredients nor the facilities for making one I had to call in outside help. Someone had told me that an electrical engineer living in Bukuru and working for the Nigerian Electrical Supply Company had previously trained as a pastry cook and sometimes made birthday and wedding cakes for friends.

I did not know Bernard and Marie Prescott but decided that I would send them a letter with the messenger when he returned to the Plateau, explaining our problem and asking if they could make the cake. When the next stores arrived the cake arrived with them. It was a magnificent cake, pink with white decorations and a gold key with '21 Today' printed on it. My main worry was to hide it from view and protect it from the many and varied insects which were prevalent at the time. When I wrote to Bernard and Marie to thank them for their kindness I did not realize that it was the start of a friendship which was to last to this day. We kept in touch with them until Bernard's death some years ago and we still write to Marie.

Bernard became Acting Head of Nigerian Electrical Supply Company (N.E.S.C.O.) and made cakes for various celebrations for different people but I do not think that any cake was ever appreciated as much as Roy Noel's twenty-first birthday cake.

The men at the camp contributed towards a gift and Len Metcalfe managed to buy a watch at the Wase market. George Connor shot a spur wing goose and I prepared this in readiness for the main course. It was really nice and a great improvement on the bustard mentioned in the earlier part of this book. Jack Hunt and 'Pop Taylor' contributed various food delicacies from their stores and we all pooled our liquor supplies. Our main trouble was keeping our activities secret from Roy, as this was to be a surprise party. However, he became suspicious when the other men spoke about going to the party at Meehans' camp. He was rather put out at not being invited, but the men teased him and said that it was probably because he had got drunk and behaved very badly at a previous party.

Eventually the big night arrived. I had gone out for a bush walk to get some wild flowers for the table and these along with the magnificent cake provided the centre piece. We had decorated the grass hut, Momo had done a good job of preparing the 'small chop', and between us we had prepared the main course and the desserts. Momo adored parties as apart from the fact that he and his family collected the leftover food, he generally received dashes of money from the guests. All I hoped was that we did not get a deluge as everything set out under the stars would have been ruined.

Roy was looking very dejected and Len Metcalfe finally said that he would go over to our camp and make enquiries. When he returned he told Roy that I had relented and that he would be welcome at the party after all.

At about a quarter to eight the guests arrived. Roy's eyes nearly popped out of his head when he saw the cake and he could scarcely believe that the party was all for him. George Connor had made a cute key of elephant grass stalks, and this together with the watch was presented to Roy as the guest of honour amid a good deal of hilarity and speech making. It was a most enjoyable evening and brightened us up considerably.

A wedding cake made by Bernard & Marie Prescott. They made the birthday cake for Roy Noel's 21st birthday.

When the party was over I gave Roy a large slice of cake to send to his parents in Cornwall. Some time later Mr and Mrs Noel came out to work in Nigeria and we had the pleasure of meeting them. They told us that Roy talked about the party for months. Actually it ran into years as during a chequered career he eventually turned up to work in Hong Kong, and called on some close friends of ours who were working there. As they had previously worked in Nigeria they heard all about the party in the Nigerian bush. In fact they confided to us later they eventually got very tired of hearing about it.

As most of the mining work was now finished and we were all awaiting news about our return to the Plateau there was more time for other activities. Tony and Gabriel left early one morning to go into elephant country. They returned later in the day with, I was pleased to say no elephant – they were a protected species. Tony said they had seen evidence of big game everywhere, as well as elephant pads. These pads were about a foot deep and the animals had pushed over many small trees and also some much larger ones. They also saw tracks of bush cows, antelope, hyena, giraffe and wart hogs. They actually saw wart hogs in their tracks, the only game visible except for a small duck which Tony shot. It looked something like a teal and was very good eating.

They also brought back two beautiful sprays of mauve orchids. They were the prettiest bush flowers that I had seen. Len Metcalfe said they were fairly common near the Niger River, but the flowers were much larger. The intermittent rains had caused a good deal of new growth including numbers of wild flowers. Sometimes some of the African labourers came on walks with me to collect new varieties. One morning Musa Kano arrived with, while not exactly 'the biggest aspidistra in the world', certainly the largest bulb that I had ever seen. Musa headed the deputation but the bulb was being carried by an African youth as a head load. The bulb belonged to a beautiful lily something like a hippeastrum but in paler colours. I planted it in a container and decided to take it back with me to the Plateau.

Musa also brought the news that once again we were having domestic trouble with the labourers. He said Musa Fort Lamy's wife was living in the village without food or clothing. Musa never had any money and he said he was sick of his wife anyway. She borrowed some clothes and came down to see me. Tony docked ten shillings from Musa's pay and I gave the girl a floral jersey dress of mine and a decent meal. She said she was going back to her own village, Jebb Jebb. At least her relatives would give her food when she arrived there. Evidently it was a satisfactory arrangement as Musa Fort Lamy announced he was glad to be rid of her. Probably the lass had similar sentiments about Musa Fort Lamy.

We had just settled the problem of Musa's wife when once again we found ourselves in the dental business. The wife of one of George Connor's staff came over to see us. She had very severe toothache. I was in favour of giving her aspirin and applying clove oil but she desperately wanted it out so after calming her down we started boiling up the pliers and preparing cotton wool swabs. While we were on leave I had been able to obtain some sulpha powder so I fervently prayed that there would be no complications. She was very brave about it and Tony did the extraction while Momo and I held the lass. After a short rest and a drink of brandy she was a different girl and went about proudly displaying her extracted tooth as a trophy. We sincerely hoped that there would be no more patients.

We then had an unscheduled visit from Rayfield. Robin Browne arrived with Dr Hobson, a geologist from London. Robin said he was returning to the Plateau immediately as he had made the journey by car and if it rained he would have no hope of driving the car over the flooded unmade road. I also gathered that he was not enamoured of the idea of a stay at the Tunga camp. A bonus from the visit was the fact that we all received mail and Robin was able to take letters back for posting.

Dr Hobson proved to be a very interesting visitor as he had lived and worked in remote parts of Burma, Siam, China, Malaya and Bulgaria. He had a wonderful fund of stories and experiences. Prior to coming to Nigeria he had visited an English friend who had lived in Casablanca for many years. She kept a cat whose favourite foods were oranges and curries – the hotter the better. I never tried these delicacies on our cats but most of the cats we had were very fond of Ovaltine and peanuts and when I was a child in Australia we had a cat which was inordinately fond of fruit cake and cooked beetroot.

Tony and Dr Hobson had a great deal to discuss professionally and it was at this time that it was discovered that someone had stolen a piece of drill core which showed about six inches of galena. The galena would have had a value of a shilling or so in the Wase market but as it had cost thousands of pounds for the drilling and was the most tangible piece of evidence regarding the viability of any future mining operations it simply had to be found. Tony called in two of our most reliable men, Musa Kano and Usman Dikwa, and he decided to contact Sarkin Wase to see whether between them the missing core could be found. When he returned he said that Sarkin Wase was quietly confident that it would be found.

About midday the next day the core was recovered. Considerable relief was felt by Tony and Dr Hobson was pleased to see the actual specimen. Evidently Musa Kano had his own ideas about who was responsible for the theft, as his suspects had been caught stealing petrol. Sarkin Wase gave the order that they were to be arrested at about 2.30 a.m. thus giving the thieves little chance of being absent from home.

The geologists now had to make up for lost time. Tony and Dr Hobson had left before dawn as they had to inspect the mine at Zurak and some old workings in the area. They arrived back late in the evening looking very tired, but they still had a good deal of work to do and the intermittent rains were making conditions very difficult. After spending some time at the Tunga Prospect they had to return once more to the Zurak mine. On this visit to Zurak they saw a large number of what appeared to be enormous tree frogs. No one seemed able to identify them.

We were all anxiously awaiting news about our return to the Plateau and hoped that the messenger would soon return with our instructions, however, there was no sign for several days of either the messenger or our stores. We had plenty of the basics – flour, tea, sugar, etc. but the drillers were getting very short of several items. Fortunately Tony had shot a roan antelope so there was plenty of meat for everyone.

As the days wore on all members at the camp were becoming very fed up. To make life more intolerable we were now plagued with myriads of insects including large numbers of sand flies. These were vicious little brutes and they made life for me almost intolerable. Others were not so viciously attacked, but I seemed to be their favourite victim. Somewhere in our stores we had a gin bottle filled with Dimp which was an excellent insect repellent. One morning when the insects were at their worst, I was sitting at the table drinking brandy and slapping on Dimp. One of the drillers called at the hut and gasped, 'If you are not careful one of these days you will be slapping brandy on yourself and drinking the Dimp.' 'Personally,' I said, 'the way I feel now I just don't give a damn.' Later I did develop sandfly fever and was quite ill from it.

Finally, the messenger and the stores did arrive. Somewhere along the route the stores had got wet and a good deal of the flour and sugar was spoilt, but all was forgiven when he told us that arrangements were now finalized for our return to the Plateau. A house had been found for Tony and me and the remaining personnel were to be housed in transit houses until their travel documents were ready and they were able to leave the country.

As we knew that this was the end of our bush tour we decided to have a farewell party. We pooled our food and drink. Dr Hobson was our guest of honour. It was a happy party and although we all got drenched on the way back to our tents nothing dampened our spirits. There was much to be done prior to our departure. The drilling machinery had to be dismantled, and the personal effects of ourselves and our African staff packed for transport. Tony went to say his farewells to Sarkin Wase. He told them he would return after the rainy season was over. Actually he did not return on October 11th. We were, of course, disappointed that not enough mineral had been discovered to make large scale mining a viable proposition. The cost of infrastructure such as electricity and good roads would have been enormous.

It was particularly disappointing to Sarkin Wase. He had given us a great deal of help and had hoped that a big discovery would have generated a great deal of prosperity for his district.

I farewelled young Ali Bashar. He was a local boy and wanted to return to his people at Bashar. I missed young Ali. He had been a great help with Ned Kelly and as he was always ready for fun was very popular with Africans of all ages.

With our return to the Plateau we knew that our exploration group would be broken up. George Connor returned to Australia, and Len Metcalfe went back to Canada. The drillers returned to their company in England and later were posted worldwide. Roy Noel went to work on the Kariba Dam and then later to Saudi Arabia and Hong Kong. Tony and Tom John returned to the Plateau to once again work with Frank Williams on the large columbite project. From there Tom John later went to work for the company in what was then known as Nyasaland and though he has worked in many places of the world since then we still remain close friends.

On a personal note I found it hard to realize that after nearly eighteen months of a nomadic life, living in tents mud huts and grass houses my primitive trekking life in Nigeria was over. Although I sometimes went with Tony on short excursions later it was never again a way of life; however it was an experience that I was never to forget. In spite of the discomfort, and at times dangerous life it was wonderfully interesting, and in this day and age when so much of the world had been so thoroughly explored I take pride in the fact that I was the first white woman to have set foot in some very isolated villages. During the two tours I had been washed out, blown out, and partially burnt out of various camps.

On leaving Tunga I made a firm resolution that no one was ever going to persuade me to take a camping holiday. It was a resolution that I have kept to this day.

The day I sailed from Australia a generous relative jokingly said, 'If you can't stand the place just send us a cable and we'll send you the return fare home.' In all the time I was out in the bush there was only once that I felt like taking up the offer, but at that time I was about seventy miles from the nearest post office! Mail was our greatest problem when we were on trek. We had to rely on the very erratic arrival of our stores from the Plateau. During the first bush tour before I arrived in Nigeria Tony and Pat Lewis had been exploring in the Bauchi Emirate and there had been some mix-up at the company canteen regarding the delivery of stores to members of the staff who were out bush and their stores had not arrived. The two months supply had dwindled to almost nothing and they were reduced to living on yams, the odd bush fowl they managed to shoot, and very little else. Pat was a heavy smoker and was not too easy to live with when he was without cigarettes.

Delivery arrangements improved greatly during the second and third tours, but there were always difficulties when we were in very remote areas. The messenger brought down mail and stores, but these were left at a base camp and carriers had to be sent to collect our supplies. Generally, before the carriers had arrived at the base the messenger had long departed for the Plateau and our mail would have to wait weeks before it was collected.

Sometimes our mail and stores did not even arrive at base camp but had to be left on the side of a track until the carriers arrived. Generally a labourer was left in charge. I was very impressed by the honesty of these people, as during our long tours the only article ever stolen was a carton of cigarettes. Admittedly the chop boxes were locked but there were always loose parcels and property with the mail. As we did not wish ever to be reduced to the situation of living on yams again I kept a locked box of 'iron-rations' – flour, yeast, sugar, salt tea, coffee, etc. and this was never opened until fresh supplies arrived.

Chapter 14

Return to the Plateau – Tin Mining

The Jos Plateau along with Malaysia and Bolivia was one of the great tin mining areas of the world, and according to historical sources tin had been smelted and traded from Northern Nigeria for a very long time. The Hausa smelters had established a guild and the tin traded evidently came from their furnaces. These furnaces were later discovered at Liruen Kano and probably there were many more scattered over the Plateau, because when we were living at Crown Bird Creek near Bukuru we found the remains of a small furnace in the bank of the creek just near our house.

The method of smelting was ingenious. The moulds were made from straws of coarse elephant grass about one foot long, tightly packed into bundles and set in damp ashes or mud. The molten metal was run off from the furnaces into these grass moulds and the resultant rods known as straw tin were traded by various routes through northern Africa to Mediterranean ports and beyond.

Articles made from pure tin have a long history, some being found in ancient Egyptian tombs. As tin ores were not found in Egypt, the tin must have been imported, but where it came from has never been recorded. The Phoenicians had been working tin deposits in Cornwall as far back as 1000 B.C. and it is possible that the Egyptians may have imported tin from these sources or it could have reached them from Northern Nigeria. There is very little documented history of the tin trade in the Mediterranean region but from time to time tin straws, eventually traced to Northern Nigerian sources were found in various Mediterranean ports. The existence of this tin had been known to the Royal Niger Company since 1885 as these tin straws had been purchased by the Niger Company Mines Department and the company were anxious to find the source of the tin which up to that time had been a well kept secret of the Hausa traders.

At the beginning of this century the Niger Company, acting on some rumours, sent two expeditions to the Plateau but no trace of tin was discovered.

However, in 1903 a European did reach the top of the Plateau. He was Colonel Laws and he arrived at Bukuru and spent Christmas there.

On the 22nd of January 1954 a Commemoration was held at the Foley Theatre, A.T.M.N., Bukuru to mark the fiftieth anniversary of the arrival of Colonel Laws and his party on the Plateau. Part of the program consisted of a recorded speech by Colonel Laws as well as reminiscences by other pioneers of tin mining on the Plateau.

Among the early European miners on the Plateau were a number of Australians who had come from the Tasmanian tin fields. Foremost among these were Col. Jim Foley who was largely responsible for the amalgamation of many of the smaller tin mines into the giant company Amalgamated Tin Mines of Nigeria, at one time the world's largest producer of tin metal. These Australian tin miners were joined by tin miners from Cornwall, Malaysia and South America.

By the time Tony went to work in Nigeria in 1949 most of the mines were managed and worked not by private miners, but by mining companies, the largest of which was A.T.M.N. Other large mining companies were Gold and Base, Bisichi and Jantar. There were also several small mines, some of them quite lucrative, worked by private miners. The mines worked by A.T.M.N. were spread over a large area of the Plateau from Rayfield in the north to below Dorowa in the south.

The company's administrative officers and most of the departmental heads worked from the Rayfield offices, while scientific personnel worked in laboratories in Bukuru. Bukuru was quite a large town as it contained the transport yard, the company stores, African and European clubs, the mine canteen known as 'the chop store', a railway station, a bus station and quite a large market.

The A.T.M.N. southern areas were administered from Barakin Ladi where the set-up was similar to that at Bukuru. The mines were opencast mines some of which could be seen from quite a distance as they were dominated by large walking draglines and huge heaps of excavated soil. Most of the workers in the mines were pagans. The pagans were the predominant people of the Plateau and several tribes were never conquered during the Fulani wars. The big mining companies set up villages for their workers. They also often had a club and a canteen but many of the pagans elected to live in their own villages. These villages, and there were dozens of them scattered over the Plateau, were generally built among large granite boulders and were protected by high hedges of cactus called karena. The karena had long, strong thorns and a densely packed high hedge copiously armed with these thorns made an almost impregnable barrier against man or animal.

Most of our life was naturally centred around the mines and the mining community and it was from there that most of the Plateau prosperity was generated, but the most important town of the Plateau was Jos. Because of its cooler and healthier climate as well as its natural beauty Jos was a favourite spot for government officials to take local leave or a short break. This was often spent at an attractive rest house set in a beautiful garden. When we returned to the Plateau after our long stint in the hot unhealthy areas of Shendam, Bauchi and Gombe I could hardly believe that we were in the same world.

Of course Jos had none of the history of Sokoto, Kano or Zaria. It was a comparatively new town and until the mining industry was established it was just a market with villages around it.

As far as I was concerned the chief joy of the whole Plateau area was the gardens. Even the main street of Jos, a far from beautiful thoroughfare was redeemed by a magnificent avenue of flame trees. When they were in full flower they presented a spectacular sight. Sadly I learned only a few weeks ago that after we left Nigeria the flame trees were all cut down.

The gardens around European houses were in most cases quite beautiful, flowering trees like the jacaranda, flame tree, frangipanni in all shades of pink, cream, apricot and red making a backdrop for roses, oleanders, gerberas, cannas, lilies and many others. Of course all these plants had grown in the gardens of Queensland, and were familiar to me, but I had not seen them in such profusion before.

After living for so long in makeshift abodes I was delighted at the idea of living in a real house again. We were told that we were to live in Rayfield. Most of the houses in this area were spacious and attractive with well kept gardens. When I saw the house which had been allotted to us I received a great shock. It was a small, pokey little place with nothing to recommend it, not even a garden. It did however have a wonderful view across the company golf links.

I then discovered the house was normally the residence of a bachelor prospector who spent most of his time away from it. At that time he was away on leave, and as it was the only available vacant house we were landed with it. Tony had to endure it for only a few days as the company sent him off on a tour to Ishiago in the Eastern Region. In many ways it was just as well as the house was definitely too small for two people.

With his departure everything seemed to go wrong. Our move coincided with the Moslem fast of Ramadan and as Momo and our steward were both Muslims the lack of sleep and the fasting made any help in the house practically non-existent. The outside of the house looked bad enough, but inside was an absolute shambles. The refrigerator, the hot water system and the septic system were all broken down.

I began to think that the best thing I could do would be to get out our kerosene tin bush oven and revert to the rudimentary toilet facilities of our bush camps. The final straw came when I tripped on a hole in the coir matting floor covering in the bedroom, went flying and cut my head on the edge of the table cum dressing-table.

I knew it was company policy that wives did not complain to the authorities but with Tony away for a period of unstated duration I decided to send a letter to the secretary and take the consequences. The secretary, a thoroughly delightful person, duly arrived on the scene and said that labourers and tradesmen would be sent to fix up the more urgent matters of sanitation and refrigeration.

While this was going on I decided to work off my frustrations by starting a garden. Momo was horrified when he saw me wielding a spade, the rake and, even worse, wheeling around manure in the wheelbarrow. By begging cuttings and bulbs from friends I soon had a small garden started. I knew that it would be useless trying to do anything on a large scale as it would not be long before the prospector returned from leave.

It was during my gardening activities that I had the unpleasant experience of being knocked over by lightning. I did know that we got terrific thunderstorms at the beginning and end of the rainy season but I did not realize just how serious the lightning threat was. Later I heard that during the war years a research station was set up to study the causes and effects of these turbulent electrical storms in the area. Every year some Africans were struck by lightning and while we were there two Europeans were killed.

Of course I should have had more sense than to have been out in the garden during an approaching storm but I was anxious to get some seedlings in before the rain. I remembered a vivid flash, whether from the lightning or from some of the electrical installations I was not too sure, but the next thing I knew I was flat on my back, and after that I had a terrific headache for the rest of the day. I did not venture into gardens during storms again.

Tony returned from the Eastern Region just a few weeks before the occupant of our house was due back from leave, so I knew it would not be long before we were packing up again. We decided that our household would not be complete without a cat so we acquired a blue grey short haired cat who was promptly named Bandit. Evidently a burglar anticipated our next move for prior to our departure we were robbed. Nothing of any great value was taken, the burglar apparently being interested only in food and drink. He cleaned out the refrigerator taking butter, milk and meat. He then turned his attention to the drinks and took everything except a bottle of brandy. Why this was left I could not quite work out as whisky, gin and rum all disappeared.

Our next move was to Shen about seven miles from Bukuru. Once again the occupant of the house was due to go on leave, and as there was a reasonable road Tony could commute to the geological department at Bukuru and from there travel to outlying areas. The house was quite pleasant, a considerable improvement on the one at Rayfield. It was built of mud, whitewashed inside and out for coolness, had interior beams painted black and was thatched. With a little imagination and innovation it could have been made quite attractive, but again we knew that our stay would be only a short one so I concentrated on tidying up the garden. I would like to have started a vegetable garden, but as I knew this would have taken a good deal of time I reluctantly dismissed the idea.

Our stay at Shen was uneventful; we had pleasant neighbours and as the rainy season had not finished I was able to catch up on much needed sewing and long overdue letter writing. I also had the opportunity of becoming better acquainted with other members of the mining community particularly the geological staff. The wife of the chief geologist and I became lifelong friends.

Our cat Bandit settled down well to life at Shen. He was a contented animal and Momo's daughters became very fond of him. However, our peace was short lived. One morning I was visiting a friend and while we were having a cup of tea a beautiful Siamese cat walked into the room. I admired the animal and told my friend that I had always wanted to own one. To my surprise she said that she could get one for me. She said that the manager of the Nigerian Electrical Supply Company bred Siamese cats. She kindly took me to the house, and that was how I first met Mrs Brace. She said that she had a number of kittens and I was taken to their quarters to see them. They were all lovely animals but one was outstandingly beautiful. She said I could take my pick and I chose the outstanding one, something I would never have done had I known that the kitten was to be a gift. I thought she sold the cats.

We named the kitten Warri Boko and he was placed in a cat basket and taken out to meet Bandit. It was hate at first sight. They fought like the traditional Kilkenny cats and by the end of five weeks Tony and I were nearly nervous wrecks, so we decided that another home would have to be found for Bandit. We were unhappy about this, but while we were searching for a new home the cats decided to settle their differences and became friends. They were great pals for years.

Strange to say the Africans never liked the Siamese as much as our other cats. Momo told me that it was because they had blue eyes. This prejudice extended to human beings as well, dark eyed people being more popular than those with blue eyes. I never knew quite where I fitted in as my eyes were green.

When the prospector returned from leave we were once again faced with the problem of where we were going to live. I was rather worried at the time as I knew that I had to face a serious operation in the near future. I had decided to have it done in Australia as we were due for long leave and it would give me a chance of seeing my relatives before entering hospital. However, if a house could not be found I decided that I would leave immediately and Tony would have to go to a transit house until he was due to go on leave.

At this stage the chief geologists's wife, Phyl Farrington, came to our assistance, and suggested that as they were going on leave we should occupy their house while they were away. I was delighted as Small Barn was one of the most pleasant houses on the mining property. It also had a magnificent garden, so for the first time since I had left Australia I was once again able to fill the house with flowers, and have fruit and vegetables to give away. The house was also close to Yelwa club and the swimming pool.

I spent most of my time in the garden, and was lucky in having one garden boy who was really interested in growing things. The other one was not so keen and generally worked at two speeds – 'Dead Slow' and 'Stop', but one day I saw him literally racing across the garden. I could not quite make out what had happened, but according to my willing helper, the garden boy was having a sleep underneath some shrubs and trees when a tree snake had fallen on him. Hence the unaccustomed action. This made me keep a more wary eye on trees and shrubs when gardening.

The garden at Small Barn had been laid out in rock terraces so I kept my eyes open for snakes. One day when I was doing some weeding I looked up and saw Warri Boko playing with a puff adder – a particularly venomous type of snake so I promptly called Usman Bima to dispatch the snake. I was worried about Warri and asked Usman if he thought Warri had been bitten. Usman just replied laconically, 'We shall soon know.' Fortunately Warri had not been bitten but it did not cure him of playing with snakes. On one occasion he jumped through the window with one and dumped it on our bed. In the end it seemed rather ironic that Bandit was the cat we lost through snakebite.

When our pleasant stay at Small Barn ended we once again went into a transit house to make preparations for our long trip back to Australia. We travelled to Lagos by train, and joined the *Elder-Dempster* ship at Apapa. As we were heading into the European winter we had a very rough trip after leaving Las Palmas, and only about a dozen of us showed up for the traditional New Year's Eve Party.

We left Tilbury on the P&O liner *Strathmore* and had a pleasant trip home via the Suez canal. It was all new and very exciting to me but Tony had travelled to England via Suez when he first joined A.T.M.N. so he spent most of his time playing deck sports and swimming. After nearly four years of arduous work in Nigeria he thoroughly enjoyed the trip and arrived in Australia looking fit and well. Actually I don't think any of our relatives had ever expected to see us again, and would hardly believe it when we told them that we would be returning to Nigeria at the end of our leave. My father understood. He had lived in Africa and loved it.

Unfortunately my stay in hospital was much longer than anticipated and Tony had to return to Nigeria alone while I was still a patient. There had been a change in company policy and where possible air travel had now to be used instead of travel by sea, so he flew to Rome and from there boarded a plane for Kano and Jos in Northern Nigeria.

In order to recover my health it was suggested that I travel to England by sea and then make a further sea voyage to Lagos. I returned to England on the same ship as I had left five months previously, the *Strathmore*. After two weeks in England I set out for Rotterdam to join a Dutch cargo-passenger ship sailing for Lagos. We called at several ports in Europe and Africa and in spite of, or perhaps because of, the diversity of nationalities and professions we had a very happy voyage.

My old friend Mr Shoda met me in Lagos and told me that a new hotel had been built, and there would be none of the chaos which attended my first arrival in the country. As usual he was wonderfully helpful and even made arrangements for an appointment for me at the hairdresser's. It was just as well as I would have had a great deal of trouble trying to find the place by myself. When I was leaving he took me to Iddo Junction to join the up-country train for Jos and gratefully accepted the cartons of American cigarettes I had got for him in Monrovia.

Chapter 15

The Columbite Boom – Life at Zawan

During our absence in Australia there had been a great deal of activity in the mining company. With all the work to be done on the columbite project more staff had been recruited and a building programme had been put under way, so that there were now more houses for the staff.

Just after my return friends of ours told us that they intended leaving and that the husband was due to take up a position with the Mines Department in Hong Kong. We had always liked their house although by Plateau standards it was in a lonely situation near a large pagan settlement at Zawan. For this reason it was not a popular residence, and when Jean and John said that they would be leaving the company and we said that we would be happy to take over their house we had little competition for it. Once again we were back with pagan neighbours this time with the Biroms.

The house was situated on a large compound and one of the former occupants had made some attempt at starting a garden. A few old fashioned roses, oleanders, and frangipanni were still surviving. Along with the garden I acquired a new garden boy, Tete, who was a Tiv. I knew nothing of the Tiv tribe but Tony had met some of them when he had been down in the Eastern Region. He said that the Tivs were an industrious and intelligent people, but the men were well known for their fondness for beer, imported or the local home brew known as Pito.

Although Tete's knowledge of gardening was rudimentary he had a natural flair for it, learnt quickly and became a great help in setting up a vegetable garden and helping me with the heavier tasks. At the weekends he went in for riotous living and on Monday morning generally arrived looking very ill and suffering from a monumental hangover. At first I tried to cure these with Alka-Selzer and Prairie oysters, but then decided that more economical methods would have to be adopted, so every Monday morning Tete would start the day with a mug of water to which I had added a large spoonful of bicarbonate of soda. It no doubt tasted horrible but worked wonders for Tete, and he was always asking me for what he called 'powerful medicine'.

One of the first things which we planted in our new garden was an avocado pear tree. I knew that we would not be in the house long enough to get any fruit, but I made it a practice to plant an avocado tree in any house garden that we occupied. They took years to fruit but some eventually yielded crops. Momo would sometimes come home with a quantity of the pears. I never knew where he got them until I later discovered that he went around to the houses we had occupied and informed the then residents that Madame had planted and looked after the tree. They generally accepted his story and gave him some of the fruit. As I have mentioned before, Momo was a great charmer.

Although we did not see very much of our pagan neighbours we were plagued by their herds of goats. Tete and I had no way of fencing off the vegetable garden and a hedge was going to take a considerable time to grow. The flower garden was more or less protected by a thick hedge of oleander, (poisonous to people and animals) and another low hedge of very prickly euphorbia.

One morning I received a great surprise to see a deputation of pagans coming down the drive with the leader carrying what I thought was a dog but on closer inspection proved to be a dead goat. Momo and Tete joined the gathering and after considerable shouting and carrying on I learned that the pagans had accused our dog of killing the goat, and they were demanding compensation, and as the goat was pregnant the normal compensation claim was doubled. Tony had lived through all this before when he was working on the Kagoro plateau and a friend's dog had worried a goat, pregnant of course, and finally compensation had been agreed upon.

The Biroms had evidently decided that this was a good scheme for getting a little extra cash, and had no doubt tried the idea out on other Europeans. In our case they were rather unfortunate as we were one of the few European families on the Plateau that did not keep a dog. The pagan deputation was then treated to a round of invective in Hausa, English and Tiv from Momo, Tete and myself. Probably they did not understand much of what was being said but our tone was unmistakable, and it was some time before we saw the pagans or their goats again.

While we were living at Zawan I joined the Plateau Horticultural Society, and remained a member until I left Nigeria. The society gave advice on the establishment and maintenance of gardens and was very useful to those unfamiliar with tropical and sub-tropical gardening. It had published a book on gardening on the Plateau and every year at the end of June the annual Plateau Horticultural Show was held. This was the big event of the year for gardeners, European and African. It was well patronized and some years there were very fine floral exhibits, particularly from the well established gardens. Tete revelled in these shows and for weeks prior to the event gave me a great deal of enthusiastic help getting things ready.

Because of its isolated situation the house at Zawan was particularly vulnerable to robbery. The house had an outside kitchen and the first casualty was our entire kitchen equipment. All the pots, pans, kettles etc. vanished, but fortunately the one thing the company could not replace, my Australian egg beater, the thieves threw away. It turned up in the vegetable garden so this useful piece of equipment was salvaged. Evidently the night watchman or maigardi was asleep while the robbery was perpetrated.

We decided to move the maigardi to a more strategic position and hoped that in any future robberies that he would play a more active role. We did not have long to wait. After the success of the kitchen raid they decided to rob the store. As the house was made of mud brick some tunnelling under the barred store window was undertaken. While this was going on apace the thieves did not realize that they were being observed by a wide awake maigardi, and just as they were about to get the store window out the maigardi took a pot shot at one of the thieves with his large bow and arrow. It was a lucky hit, striking the thief fair and square in the buttocks. The would be robber let out a blood curdling yell and the whole enterprise was abandoned. The maigardi gave Tony a graphic account next morning, and his only regret seemed to be that the poison on the arrow might be too old. After this episode we were not troubled by thieves again.

The village at Zawan was the centre of a Catholic mission, and we became very friendly with the sisters and fathers at the mission. They ran a school and a hospital as well as a church, and attended to the spiritual and material needs of a very large community. I became very friendly with one of the sisters who was in charge of the hospital. I was now assured that in the event of illness our domestic staff would be well cared for. They attended to some of the childish complaints of Momo's daughters and as the years went by and the girls married I made sure that their babies were born at the hospital. Even when we moved to our house at Crown Bird Creek they still attended the hospital at Zawan. They much preferred it to the African hospital in Jos. Tony's old headman Musa Kano had been a patient at Jos hospital and had not been happy there. When I went to see him he asked me not to leave the bag of food and comforts we had prepared for him as he said that he would not see any of it but he would come to our place and collect it when he left hospital.

When Momo's daughter, Dada Karima, was married she went with her two children to visit her sister in Southern Nigeria. On the way back to the plateau there was evidently an epidemic of measles and the three of them took very ill on the train. Sadly her toddler died and by the time Dada reached us she was very ill indeed and we thought that the poor girl, little more than a child herself, would die before we could get her to hospital. However, Tony drove them straight to the Zawan hospital and Sister saved both Dada Karima and her baby. Momo was always grateful for the treatment that they received, and when the sisters occasionally came to lunch nothing was too much trouble for him to prepare. They were certainly some of his favourite guests.

It was not only people that we were looking after. As previously mentioned we never kept a dog of our own when we were in Nigeria, but we frequently looked after other people's animals when their owners were on leave so we generally had extra cats and sometimes dogs in our care. Our main reason for not having a dog of our own was the fact that the terrible disease rabies was very prevalent in the country. The Vom veterinary station did an excellent service in rabies control and provided anti-rabies injections for animals. Our cats were always taken to Vom for inoculation and it was obligatory for owners of dogs to have them inoculated. However, there was always the danger of pi-dogs invading the compound and of course bush animals such as monkeys were also susceptible to the disease. Almost every year there was a rabies scare. It was a horrifying disease and the treatment was drastic, a long course of painful injections. At first these were all given in the stomach but later the injections were more widely distributed over the body.

One Sunday we were invited to a friend's house for a curry lunch, but during the week we had made arrangements for a bush picnic. As far as we were concerned it was a fortunate decision, as while the lunch was in progress a rabid dog came into the house and all the guests had to attend the hospital to go through the long and painful course of injections. We were very lucky in that during our long stay in the country we never came into contact with a rabid animal.

Apart from dogs and cats we also looked after other pets. Many people kept West African grey parrots and when some friends asked us to look after 'Aku' I said that I did not know much about parrots, but as their routine appeared to be very simple I decided to welcome him as a temporary member of our family. We became very fond of Aku and when he was handed back to his owners we missed him so much that Tony decided to give me one for a birthday present. It was a delightful bird but it did not talk very much.

Parrots were, of course, very popular, and I came home from Jos one day to find that the bird had disappeared and no doubt was promptly resold. We soon had a replacement, and Rudolf, as he was called, became part of the family. He was a wonderful talker and learnt new words and phrases very quickly. We always taught him to say, 'Merry Christmas' to greet our visitors at Christmas time. Of course he continued his greeting long past the festive season. As his predecessor had vanished from his outdoor perch Rudolf spent a good deal of his time indoors.

I worried about his being in a small cage inside so Tony decided to get a very large cage built so that he could be put in it on the back lawn. We referred to it as his country residence and expected him to love it. When he was put inside it he promptly left it and walked back into his small cage and never used the country house again except under sufferance.

If we had guests of an evening he would spend a good deal of time calling out, 'I'm Rudolf Meehan. Who are you?' Then he would call out a list of names. A friend who was knowledgeable about birds said a parrot should not do this but should be kept quiet at night covered with a dark cloth. I made a black poplin cover, pulling it over the cage and Rudolf had a wonderful fifteen minutes tearing it to pieces.

When the time came to leave Nigeria we hated parting with him, but Australian quarantine regulations were extremely strict regarding the import of caged birds and Rudolf was very definitely a prohibited migrant. Sadly we left him with a New Zealand friend, but we missed our friend Rudolf very much.

There were, of course, sometimes disasters in looking after pets. My luck rain out when I promised to take care of a friend's beautiful aquarium of tropical fish. My knowledge of fish maintenance was virtually nil, but after a few instructions it seemed tolerably simple and for a while the fish thrived. One night, however, I forgot to cover the tank while the room was being sprayed against mosquitoes and next morning the aquarium was finished. I hardly knew how to face the owner on his return, but when I next went on leave I managed to get some replacements. They travelled out in a large glass jar in my cabin on my return journey to Lagos, but this was my first and last experience with tropical fish for aquariums.

I also pre-dated the Russians by putting an animal into orbit. Two years before Yuri Gagarin and his dog made their sensational flight we were looking after Eileen Corby's cat. It developed a nasal complaint and never seemed to stop sniffing and sniffing. One of our geological friends had a similar complaint and he had left a bottle of nasal drops at our house so I decided on a treatment for the cat. I'll never know exactly what happened but after one application the cat took off, became virtually airborne and did a couple of orbits around the lounge before finally collapsing on the floor. I was quite sure the cat had expired, but fortunately it recovered and was permanently cured of its sniffles.

One group of animals that I flatly refused to look after or have as pets were monkeys. Tony had one on his first bush tour, but admitted that they could never be house trained. They were definitely outdoor animals and if they came inside the house created absolute havoc. Friends of ours kept two small ones as pets and one morning one came into the lounge. The first thing he pounced on was a glass of sherry. The sherry was emptied on to the carpet and the glass was thrown after it. The monkey then sneaked along the back of my chair and promptly removed a pearl necklace I was wearing. It then took up a position on a tall indoor plant and went on playing with my necklace. We had quite a bit of trouble getting it away from him.

A few people kept larger animals as pets, but I never liked to see animals like cheetahs and bush cats confined in small areas. One animal which no one should have kept as a pet was a leopard. Although they were beautiful little animals when they were small they were never meant to be domestic pets. There was an incident in Jos in 1952 which made headlines in the *Nigerian Citizen* and certainly emphasised the danger of keeping leopards as pets.

The following is the account of the incident as reported in the *Nigerian Citizen* of April 10th 1954:

MISSIONARY SAVES A.D.O. IN FIGHT WITH LEOPARD

JOS 'PET' KILLS ONE, INJURES SIX

An S.I.M. missionary punched and kicked a maddened pet leopard as it lay on top of a Jos A.D.O., mauling him. The leopard, which had been kept in a cage by Malam Kolo of the health department, killed one African and injured two more Africans, two A.D.O.s, a European police officer, an S.I.M. missionary and an African police corporal before it was finally killed. As soon as the leopard broke out from his cage he attacked the first people he saw, a party of three Africans who happened to be passing nearby. One of the Africans has since died and the others are in hospital.

A group of people then chased the leopard on to a rocky hill at the north end of the town. Forty year old John Vaughan and three missionaries went to the hill where they saw the leopard crouching in a hole. Vaughan opened fire with his rifle and the leopard charged around the back of the rock and leaped on him before he could get up. Mr Nicholls, a missionary, then jumped forward and punched the leopard in the face with his fist and kicked it in the stomach. The leopard turned on Mr Nicolls who received lacerations to his shoulder and leg before the leopard retreated to its hole. Vaughan had been badly clawed on the shoulder and back. The two remaining missionaries took the wounded men to hospital, and a senior Supt. of Police, two European officers, a D.O., an A.D.O. and a P. & T. engineer armed with rifles then took up the attack. Two shots were fired at the leopard and again it came out of its lair, attacking twenty-six year old A.D.O., John Greig, who was badly clawed on the shoulder and face. Gripping the leopard's throat Greig managed to force it away and it turned on Asst. Supt. C.J.M. Patterson who placed his rifle across his body to protect himself, but the speed of the leopard's attack threw him off the ledge twenty feet to the ground. The leopard's paw nearly tore off Patterson's ear as he fell. Yet again the leopard retreated to his lair and reinforcements were summoned. Armed with rifles, bayonets and shot guns a party of Europeans arrived at the scene.

This time shots would not move the leopard and a courageous African climbed the rock and prodded the leopard out of his hole with a bamboo pole. As it charged out Mr Sharland of U.A.C. fired quickly and the leopard swerved, obviously hit, and leaped on to an African police corporal. Just as the leopard was about to savage the man John Bull in charge of Jos Division opened fire and brought the leopard to the ground.

Had it not been for the seriousness of the attack the whole thing could have formed the plot of a third rate movie. However, after the episode I don't think either Africans or Europeans kept leopards as pets.

A leopard story with a much happier ending concerned one of the young prospectors working with A.T.M.N. David was returning home from work one evening and chancing to look behind saw a leopard trotting along the path a few paces behind him. It was in the Richa area at a spot where leopards were occasionally seen. I rather gathered from David that he quickened his pace and fortunately when he turned off the path to his camp the leopard just continued along the path and made no attempt to follow him.

There were a couple of other reported cases where people were mauled but this generally happened only when the animal was cornered. One of our geological visitors, Dr Prigogine, told us that his right arm had been torn by a leopard while he was working in the Belgian Congo but fortunately in spite of dreadful lacerations the wound did not become septic as was usually the case as leopard claws were usually infected with germs from carrion meat.

Chapter 16

Housekeeping on the Plateau – Home Delivery

When I left Australia supermarkets and shopping centres were still un-known. One or two chain stores such as Crofts or Dickens did operate, but most of our food orders, baker, butcher, grocer etc. were still home delivered. I soon discovered that home delivery in Nigeria was somewhat different to home delivery in Australia.

My first caller was the milkmaid, a very attractive young Fulani girl balancing a calabash of milk on her head. The milk was a rather dubious looking fluid which brought to my mind the old rhyme which we used to recite as children:

I never saw a purple cow. I never hope to see one,
But from the milk we're getting now, I'm sure that there must be one.

I purchased some of this milk and promptly boiled and cooked it. When Tony arrived home he said, 'Give it to the cats and for heaven's sake don't drink it.' Milk was evidently diluted with various products, the best of which was water from odd sources and if sour milk was required cow's urine was sometimes added. After these revelations I decided to rely on tinned and powdered milk, but my little Fulani friend continued to call on me.

Until our vegetable gardens became productive a gentleman clad in a leather belt and very little else would sometimes call with potatoes and fruit. One of his first offerings was a bunch of enormous bananas. He was so keen to sell these, and kept showing me what wonderful bananas they were. He was rather taken aback when I said, 'They are not really bananas. They are plantains but I will buy some to bake.' Most of the residents of the Plateau had come from the colder parts of Europe where bananas and plantains did not grow. Anyway, he was delighted that I knew what they were and promptly offered two of them as a 'dash'.

Eggs were always a problem and following the general custom I always met the egg vendor with a dish of water to test for comparative freshness. Any that floated were definitely unacceptable. However, there were traps even with what appeared to be the freshest eggs. One day my friend Jean called and said she had been lucky enough to get two dozen eggs all of which appeared to be fresh. I was rather surprised but not nearly so surprised as Jean was when she came to use them. The trader making sure that they would all sink had hard boiled the lot.

Momo took a rather poor view of these back door traders and said that he could get much better things at the market in Bukuru. He generally did, and the small amount of market money he received as a dash fully compensated for the time he had to spend haggling over the price and quality. He loved going to market, but even then things did not always go smoothly. One day I went into the kitchen to find the usually good natured and smiling Momo positively fuming and growling about the awful onions Madame had bought and which he couldn't peel. I couldn't understand this as I never bought onions and always relied on Momo getting good quality onions at the market.

When I went into the store the mystery was solved. When our annual horticultural show was held I had admired some magnificent gladioli grown by one of the Judges in Jos. When he lifted the corms he was kind enough to present me with some and these were the 'onions' which Momo had discovered. I was very thankful that only two of the corms had been mutilated. We had a good laugh over this and I teased him about his onion shopping.

Whenever we moved house some of our first visitors were Hausa traders. They generally wore the traditional Hausa gown or riga and carried their goods in leather bags or wrapped in the ever useful mat. Sometimes they came alone but generally one or two small boys staggering under huge loads of trade goods came with them.

The goods usually consisted of leather bags made from crocodile, snake or goat skin, as well as leather photo frames, brass trays, beads, praying mats, wooden carvings and sometimes articles made from ivory. All this was spread out and then the bargaining began. If you had a good deal of time on your hands the bargaining was rather fun as it took quite a while to get down to the 'last price'. If you did not have much time it could be something of a hassle. The trader always looked a bit disappointed if you did not join in the bargaining, and if you paid the first asking price I think they thought you were crazy.

Over the years I got to know some of the traders very well and when I was finally leaving the country a dear old man who used to trade outside Chellerams in Jos and was always trying to sell me something, from wristlet watches to pickling onions, came to the airport to see me off and as a farewell 'dash' gave me a string of homemade green beads. I still have this necklace, and wear it quite often.

Of course most of our shopping was done through the company canteen better known as the 'chop store'. Every two or three weeks each household sent their grocery order and a large wooden 'chop box' to the canteen. The order was then packed, the box locked and delivered.

The lady in charge was ruthlessly efficient and stood no nonsense from anyone. Regarding your order it was necessary to cultivate a good memory, because if any item was forgotten you could not get it until the next order and if you could not borrow from a friend you did without. Things became a little easier when the stores in Jos began to carry a wider range of products.

Naturally not all culinary disasters concerned marketing. Most of the disasters occurred in the kitchen. Our household was no exception. A volume could be written about odd meals, burnt meals and at times no meals at all and there were times when the origin of the dinner was shrouded in mystery. Perhaps it was better so.

When we returned from long sessions in the African bush we generally went out to a number of dinners, cocktail parties, and other social events, mainly to see friends and hear the news of the past months. At one drinks party the hostess became rather suspicious at the number of anchovy savouries that kept appearing. She went into the kitchen and reappeared looking rather worried, and I did notice that we had no more savoury titbits with our drinks. It was weeks later that I learned that the cook had run out of anchovy paste and had spread the remainder of the cracker biscuits with tinned cat food. Fortunately as most of the guests had imbibed a fair amount of liquor they had not noticed anything peculiar about the savouries. No one seemed to suffer any harmful after effects.

There was one particularly memorable dinner held on Saint Patrick's day. We were not guests but the host, an Irishman, invited all his Irish friends and as a patriotic gesture to the lady guests had made arrangements for each of them to be presented with a bouquet of shamrocks. These had been sent out by air for the occasion. When the time came for the presentation they were told that they had already had the shamrocks – in the soup! Cook had decided that they were a special kind of spinach. It was definitely an interesting variation on the traditional Irish stew.

It was always rather difficult to get guests to the table. Many seemed more interested in liquid refreshment than in a meal. African cooks were very clever at keeping food hot and edible for long periods of time, but I did not have this skill. As a special treat I decided on a Bombe Alaska as a dessert, but as I could not manage to get my guests to the table at the appropriate time all they got was a nasty mess of soggy sponge and melted ice cream. From that time on I concentrated on dishes that would not spoil with keeping – soufflés were definitely out.

One morning the then chief geologist's wife called on me. We had dined with her the previous evening and she asked me if I had noticed anything queer about a lemon meringue pie we had eaten as dessert. I said that the filling did appear a little lumpy, but I did not take much notice as this could so easily happen. She then said that the lumps were actually tinned crab. She had given her cook tinned crab to make fish cocktails. This was evidently something new to the cook, so he minced the crab and added it to the lemon filling. Definitely a new taste sensation.

It was not only the meal courses which could be somewhat unexpected, you never knew whose dishes they were going to be served on. Many times I ate off my own dinner plates at other people's houses and dinner parties. If the stewards thought you were running short of cutlery or china they just slipped across to the nearest neighbour and borrowed the articles. The steward I had prior to Suli was not particularly enterprising and evidently did not think of borrowing extra china from our nearest neighbours and one morning I was inspecting the kitchen before a dinner party when I noticed mixed up with plates from the dinner set were some odd looking dishes. The extra number had been made up with three or four enamel plates left over from our second bush tour.

Apart from not knowing where your dishes were likely to come from there were times when we did not know who our guests would be. One afternoon I arrived home to find a German geologist, a young Englishman and a small girl sitting in our lounge. As we had promised to attend a function in Jos in the evening to farewell a close friend who was leaving the country I had a hurried consultation with Suli and decided that I would have to set up a cold table for the guests and leave them to their own devices until we returned. The German geologist was not staying overnight but beds had to be found for the young Englishman and his daughter.

In the excitement of getting the food ready, trying to get ourselves organized for the cocktail party and fixing up accommodation I completely forgot about the child, a dear little girl who was 'touring' with her father. Anyway Suli did a wonderful job in my absence. He prepared the little girl a supper of scrambled eggs, toast and marmite and then made up a bed for her on a mat so that she could be near her father. He then carefully tucked the mosquito net around the bed and the mat. I did not enquire into the circumstances of why such a young child was being subjected to what must have been a rather hazardous life. Anyway both men seemed to have enjoyed their evening and I noticed that there was very little left of a substantial pork pie and other delicacies, and they were chatting away quite happily when we returned home.

Even organizing meals on the Plateau was not easy at times. I did not, of course have to resort to the measures I had sometimes used on our bush treks. In the bush when we were short of vegetables I had to find substitutes to keep us healthy. I found that pumpkin runners sliced made a tolerable substitute for green beans, while green pawpaws could have their seeds removed and be stuffed with almost anything, left-over chicken, rice or meat, and when baked made an acceptable savoury change. I would not say that curried yams (I adapted the recipe from an old Indian recipe for curried potatoes) was a gourmet's delight, but it was a change and better than nothing when served with chutney and other relishes.

Only once did we have 'millionaire's cabbage' as I did not approve of the destruction of a whole palm tree for just one meal.

We did not, of course, have to resort to these measures on the Plateau but there was never very much meat available and much of what we got was often very tough and tasteless. Later, we were able to get lamb imported from New Zealand but it was rather too expensive to appear on the day to day menu. One great help was the company piggery. This had been started during the war years by the wife of the then General Manager of A.T.M.N. As a result we received issues of bacon, pork and sausages at fairly frequent intervals. As our staff were Muslims I generally handled these meats myself but if Momo had sometimes to deal with them I always gave him scented soap to wash his hands if he had handled pig meat. I knew he adored scented soap so there was never any trouble.

There were times when I had to serve goat meat instead of lamb or mutton. Most people did not seem to notice much difference. I suppose all this was good training as my friends often tell me today that I could make a meal out of anything.

Chapter 17

The Move to Crown Bird Creek

As the years went on there were the inevitable changes in the company structure: John Farrington left the Geological Department to become the General Manager of A.T.M.N.; Frank Williams took over as Chief Geologist and did excellent work with his geological staff until his retirement in 1958. He later went on to pursue a brilliant career in England which culminated with the award of the Gold Medal of the Institute of Mining and Metallurgy for his work on alluvial geology and mining.

With his retirement Tony was appointed Chief Geologist with the company. We knew that this would involve leaving the house at Zawan as he would have to be close to the head office at Rayfield. Most of the departmental heads lived in Rayfield, but there was a house at Crown Bird Creek half way between Bukuru and Rayfield that had always interested us.

When I first arrived in Nigeria there was a small whitewashed mud house in the compound which was not occupied by anyone in the company. I wondered who lived there and was later told that Dr Miller made his home there while he was away from Kano. Dr Miller and his sister Ethel were among the first Christian missionaries to enter Nigeria. Apart from his teaching and his missionary work he also adopted a number of boys and educated them. However, he is probably best known for his translation of the Bible into Hausa. Dr Miller's Bible translation was sometimes used as a text book by people studying for their Hausa examinations. I never met Dr Miller but Tony did during his first tour of the country.

After Dr Miller's death a new house was built on the site, but fortunately the compound was left in its original state. Some earlier residents had planted a large number of fruit trees in the garden. There were oranges, grapefruit, guavas, mangoes, pawpaws and a lemon tree. They were all in a sadly neglected state, but I thought that with pruning, fertilizing and watering they could soon be in production as the original trees seemed to have been of good stock.

Prior to moving into the house at Crown Bird Creek we went on leave and took a short holiday in Yugoslavia. It was a very interesting experience as we were some of the first tourists to enter the country after the Second World War. We entered Yugoslavia by way of Austria. After considerable trouble with the customs (mainly because of the number of cameras carried by the tourists) we set off on the long journey. The trip was to take us through the central part of the country and back up the Dalmatian coast to the Italian border. We travelled through Slovenia, Croatia, Bosnia, Herzogovina, Serbia and Macedonia and visited the cities of Banjaluka, Zagreb, Sarajevo and Dubrovnik.

Dubrovnik was probably the most interesting. The old city was enclosed within a fortress-like wall which Tony and I walked around. As tourists were a novelty at that time we created considerable interest in some of the more isolated villages far removed from the larger cities. Life in these parts was very primitive. There were practically no motor vehicles and the people had to rely very heavily on the horse. As a result there were a large number of horse troughs scattered through the country side. At the end of some of the troughs there was a small dog trough. Once or twice when our laundry problems became acute I had to resort to washing a couple of garments in the horse trough and rinsing them out in the dog trough. I only hoped that later the horses were not blowing bubbles.

Toilet facilities were even more primitive and as a friend had given me a large bottle of a well known French perfume I generally headed the procession of tourists and sprayed the toilets out with perfume to make them slightly more acceptable. I have to admit that the wonderful French fragrance is no longer one of my favourite perfumes. We enjoyed our return journey along the Dalmation coast and regretted that the whole trip had been so rushed. However, we fell in love with the country and have returned several times since our first exciting visit. These later visits gave us more time to explore the beauties of Lake Bled and to spend more time in the historically interesting cities of Mostar, Sarajevo and Zagreb. We eventually travelled as far as we could with reasonable safety to the Albanian border.

Of course there have been millions of tourists to Yugoslavia since our first visit and we no longer created the interest that we did on that first memorable trip.

Modern hotels and tourist resorts had sprung up everywhere and one no longer indulged in such activities as laundering in horse troughs, or spraying out toilets with perfume.

On our return we moved into the house at Crown Bird Creek. We soon settled in. Momo was delighted with the set-up as his house was also new and boasted the luxury of electric light and cement floors on which he could lay his mats.

Among our first visitors were the beautiful Crown birds from which the creek got its name. The crowned crane was fairly common throughout West Africa but the largest numbers were to be found in the Northern provinces of Nigeria, Ghana and Gambia. These birds were spectacular to look at and stood about two feet high at the shoulder. The crown situated at the back of the head was really a bunch of gold coloured bristles tipped with black. The front part of the head was adorned with thick, black velvet plumes. The remainder of the plumage was dark coloured while the bill was black and the legs and feet bluish black.

These birds were often found in very large flocks and their natural habitat was the marsh lands. They were also found in the sandy beds of rivers and creeks – hence their presence at Crown Bird Creek. Unlike the large flocks seen in the marshlands they frequented the creeks in small numbers generally in pairs or groups of three although on one occasion I did see a group of five on the creek bank. As we never saw many of the birds together they did not cause any problems to the small pagan farms in the area. However the birds were grain eaters and were something of a menace along the alluvial flats of the Upper Niger where large crops of rice and millet were grown. Large flocks of birds often caused considerable damage in these areas.

I never did see the famed nuptial dance of the Crowned Cranes which according to ornithologists was a spectacular rite. From the descriptions of those who had seen it I gathered that it was very similar to the dance performed by the Australian brolgas. The large birds leapt towards each other and then retreated with their wings flapping. They then danced around each other in circles. They would then leap away to a considerable distance, turn and bound back, once again to whirl around and dance.

The creek and garden attracted an enormous number of birds and the colours and variety rivalled the glorious birdlife I had seen in outback Australia. Apart from the Crowned Cranes we were host to weaver birds, azure starlings, hammerkops, secretary birds, kingfishers, sunbirds, Abyssinian Rollers, as well as migratory birds from the colder regions of

Northern Europe. Sometimes we saw the brilliant coloured, bright green bee-eaters. They made their nests in the banks of the creek.

The compound also supported a considerable amount of wildlife, apart from the inevitable snakes, lizards and skinks. There were at various times quite a number of chameleons which I found fascinating. My Hausa friends and other Africans, Yoruba, Tiv and Pagan seemed to hate them. They did not kill them but were obviously in great awe of them.

As the country around us was dotted with granite boulders, snakes, particularly rock cobras, were always a worry to me. If we caught one I always made sure that a saucer of milk was placed outside and the maigardi was instructed to stay awake if possible. He was armed with a machete and he nearly always caught the second snake. Like the garden boy mentioned earlier I had the bad luck to have a tree snake fall on me when I was gardening, and although it was not venomous I did not like the experience. I know it will not make me popular with conservationists but I have to admit that we waged relentless war on snakes. Garden boys and domestic servants were always paid a bonus for any snake caught and killed.

Later we had a visit from a doctor friend in Jos who was an ardent herpetologist and a recognized authority on snakes. While having a drink he casually mentioned that he had several snakes in the back of his car. On further enquiry he said that one was a Gabon Viper. I nearly expired on the spot and asked him to check his reptiles and make sure that none had escaped as the last thing we wanted in the compound was a Gabon viper, one of the most poisonous snakes in Africa.

One unfortunate consequence for me occasioned by our move to Crown Bird Creek was that I lost my wonderful garden boy, Tete. Tony decided that as Tete was extremely intelligent and meticulously neat his talents could be better used doing draughting and copying in the Geological office. It meant a better job for him and as he was attending night school he progressed rapidly. However he still kept up his social life which centred mainly on consuming copious quantities of beer at the weekend, so I generally saw him every Monday morning for his hangover medicine.

One Monday morning he received an absolute bonanza. At the weekend we had won a raffle at the club, the prize was two dozen bottles of Guinness, a drink which I heartily detested and Tony was not over enthu-siastic about so Tete was presented with the prize carefully rationed to two bottles at a time. It also went into the category of powerful medicine.

Although his work at the geological office was a much better job Tete was always keen on the garden and would often help me out if any extra work had to be done. His successor, George, was a likeable youth and did not mind carting water and doing rough work, but George definitely did not have green fingers. After our usual planting of an avocado tree our next job was to prune and fertilize the fruit trees. We could not do much about the mango trees. Nigerian mangoes were mostly a very stringy variety with a pronounced flavour of turpentine. Momo picked out some of the best of the fruit and traded it in the Bukuru market and the remainder of the crop was given to the pagans who lived nearby. Sometimes I made chutney with a few of the fruit as in chutney the turpentine flavour was lost, and before we were able to get canned apples they were sometimes used as an apple substitute as the addition of lemon juice could also disguise the turpentine flavour.

Another big job in the garden was the planting of a hedge around the compound. The plant selected was oleander. This shrub had several advantages as a hedge. Apart from the highly ornamental and strongly perfumed flowers in shades of pink, red and white, the plant was highly poisonous and acted as a deterrent to the goats from the pagan farms nearby.

One of the pleasures of going to live at Crown Bird Creek was that we again had Bob Hurley as a near neighbour. It was over seven years since we had set out on our long bush trek together. After leaving A.T.M.N. Bob had worked for several other mining companies on the plateau. Needless to say we visited each other fairly frequently and had a very happy time recalling many of our bush experiences. Later Bob's wife and daughter came to join him and I had the pleasure of introducing them to Nigeria. We had been on leave and Tony had flown back to the Plateau while I had decided to return by sea. While we were in London we had a note from Bob telling us that his wife and daughter would be travelling on the same ship.

It was a particularly rough trip and while I have always been lucky in being a very good sailor Brigida and Alice Hurley were not, so I did not see them until after we had left Las Palmas. Alice was a Portuguese national and did not speak English and this led to a great deal of confusion at the customs and immigration. By this time Mr Shoda's son was looking after me. He was new to the job and Alice was the first European that he had met that did not speak English. The best way I could describe it to him was that we belonged to different 'tribes'. Anyway, young Mr Shoda was just as helpful as his father and after a hair raising taxi drive through the Lagos traffic we finally reached the Mainland Hotel. After the long rail journey to Jos on the Plateau we settled down in our respective houses and remained firm friends. Momo, doing his usual good job of public relations, frequently visited the Hurleys, and I noticed that when he went over to the house he generally took a bunch of parsley with him. We grew a lot of the herb and I concluded that Alice must have been very fond of it. It was some time later that I discovered that she was paying Momo sixpence or a shilling a bunch for it. He always said she was a very nice madame although she spoke no English. I don't know just how they communicated for although Momo spoke fluent English and a smattering of Arabic as well as his native Hausa he definitely did not speak Portuguese.

Even after Bob and Alice Hurley retired and returned to Portugal we still remained firm friends and when they were living in Mateus, (centre of the wonderful rosé wine) we visited them and spent a few days with them. After their deaths we kept in touch with their daughter Brigida now happily married and living in England.

When we moved to our new house we acquired a new steward, Suli. He was a highly intelligent boy, in fact an absolute treasure. Unless we were entertaining he had a great deal of spare time so I suggested that he make a garden near the creek and sell some of the produce at the Bukuru market. We got some good seeds of tomatoes, sweet corn and beans. Suli worked hard and it was not long before he was making a good deal of cash trading at the market and among our European friends. While not himself interested in gardening or farming Momo was impressed by the extra money Suli was earning and he finally decided to start a small farm. However, he made sure that it was situated where no one would see him working in it and he offered various bribes to some of the pagans to do the digging and fertilizing. He grew cassava, yams, ochra and some herbs. His daughters set up a small roadside stall outside our back gate and sold garden produce along with matches, cigarettes, African porridge and other trade goods. The girls were very nice looking with outgoing personalities and they did quite well as their stall was on the main road between Rayfield and Bukuru.

One aspect of horticulture on which Momo was very knowledgeable was on the subject of herbs and African medicine. When we were in bush one of the labourers was bitten by a scorpion and was in extreme pain. I was applying ammonia and the old fashioned bluebag and dosing him with aspirin without much remedial effect. Tony appealed to Momo, who produced some native herb mashed it up and rubbed the bite with it. The patient got considerable and almost immediate relief. I asked him about bush medicine but he said I would only laugh. I assured him that I would not laugh at him and told him that I was always anxious to learn about herbal remedies. Later he showed me a tree the leaves and bark of which when boiled provided a concoction which was an excellent cure for malaria. The concoction was very bitter and the tree which looked like an acacia must have had some affinity with the cinchona tree from which quinine is derived.

Momo, his wife and daughters all had beautiful teeth. One reason for this was that none of them chewed cola nut, and secondly they cleaned their teeth with something known as the toothbrush plant. I also noticed that Momo had very good skin which for his age was rather unusual as most of the men and women of his age had skins badly marked by smallpox scars.

Evidently when young he had undergone some form of primitive vaccination. He said it was widely practised in his tribe and was usually done by the tribal medicine man or by one of the tribal elders. The procedure was to take pus from a pustule of someone with the disease, using a splinter or thorn to puncture the skin and vaccinate the patient. Momo said this vaccination had been practised in his tribe for a long time but I suspected that it may have been post-Jenner and possibly learnt from some medical missionary.

By the time we arrived in Nigeria most vaccination was done at clinics, dispensaries or hospitals so that smallpox was fairly well controlled. Sometimes sporadic outbreaks did occur but these were promptly dealt with by the medical authorities.

One thing which surprised me very much was the prevalence of leprosy in the country. I had never seen a case previously and thought of it as a disease mentioned in the Bible and not often seen in modern times. I was soon to be disillusioned.

Dr Barden's hospital at Vom did a wonderful job treating sick Africans, particularly those suffering from leprosy. Many of his patients walked for miles to receive treatment at his hospital. The whole hospital operated on a shoestring budget, but the amount of health care and attention was quite incredible.

Chapter 18

Social and Sporting Life

I was always amazed at the diversity of interests and hobbies displayed by the people living on the Plateau. The European community was a relatively small one, but a wide variety of sport and entertainment catered for almost every taste. This all had to be done by various people.

The only imported entertainment we had were the picture shows at the A.T.M.N. Yelwa club and at the local theatre in Jos. The films shown at the company theatre were usually of ancient vintage, while at the Jos theatre you never knew whether the dialogue was likely to be in English, Arabic or Hausa. Under these circumstances the cinema was not our most popular form of entertainment. However, there was a very active amateur theatrical society known as Yelwa Players.

Every year the Yelwa Players put on two or three plays and the big event of the year was the annual Christmas pantomime. The pantomime was a co-operative effort by most of the company personnel as well as willing helpers from Jos, the Vom veterinary station, private miners and anyone else who was prepared to help. Apart from the producer and the cast people were needed to make and paint scenery, look after the lighting and electrical equipment, assist in the orchestra, work behind the scenes, as well as design and make the dozens of necessary costumes.

We were fortunate in that there was a good deal of dancing talent in the community, but we were not so lucky with singers and the vocal talent was always the weakest feature of the shows. My contribution to the effort was the designing and making of the numerous hats and head-dresses. Over the years I must have made dozens of these. Some of the most successful pantomimes produced were *Cinderella*, *Red Riding Hood* and *Aladdin*. For a short time there were small theatrical companies in Jos and at Vom veterinary station. These added to the variety of entertainment.

106

Christmas was always a happy time as most people went to a lot of trouble to make it a joyous occasion for the children, particularly those who had come out from boarding school for the holiday period to be with their parents and families. There were parties and dances, and apart from the Sallah at the end of Ramadan there was nothing that Momo and his family enjoyed so much as Christmas and Christmas parties.

On Christmas Eve many people went to church and Midnight Mass, and the service at St Piran's Anglican church was popular with all denominations and those of no denomination. We generally went back to see our old friends the sisters and priest at Zawan mission. It always seemed to me to be the nearest one could experience to that first Christmas. The sisters always built a little crib of straw and the church was a mud edifice with a thatched roof. When we came out into the cold night air (it got quite cold at night in December) and saw the bright stars in the dark sky and the faint outlines of sheep, cattle, goats and donkeys in the surrounding African villages it must have been as close as one could get to Christmas in Bethlehem.

New Year was traditionally celebrated at the Ladi club in the southern areas of A.T.M.N. A fancy dress ball was the main feature of the celebrations and at midnight a large bonfire was lit and everyone toasted everyone else for a Happy New Year.

One of the most interesting societies was the Jos Branch of the Nigerian Field Society.

Lectures were given by various people, some residents of the plateau, some by people visiting Jos from other parts of Nigeria and occasionally some from overseas. A wide variety of subjects was covered mostly about wild life, plants, animals, reptiles, birds, but also included were archaeological and anthropological discussions as well as items of general interest. We attended many excellent lectures, the two I remember best being a lecture given by the famous anthropologist, Sir Mortimer Wheeler who happened to be visiting Nigeria at that time and another by one of our local identities, Neville Priestly. Neville was a private miner, but in his younger days had made a trip up the Amazon with Peter Fleming. This journey was well documented in Fleming's book, but Neville treated us to some of the hilarious aspects of the trip not mentioned in Fleming's book.

Unfortunately I was on leave when Mrs Leith Ross gave her lecture. Mrs Leith Ross was one of the first white women to arrive in Northern Nigeria. Before she could enter the country she first had to obtain permission from Sir Frederick (later Lord) Lugard and in 1907 she joined her husband. Sadly, her husband died of blackwater fever in 1908. After his death she returned to England but kept up her Nigerian interests by studying the Fulani, their language and customs and in 1926 she was appointed Lady Supervisor of Education. She held this position until 1937 when she was invalided home but continued her research work on Nigeria and later returned to work at Lagos and Jos museums. It was during her work at Jos Museum that I met this incredible lady.

Apart from the lectures the Field Society also provided us with some interesting excursions. There were several keen ornithologists among the members so we went on bird watching expeditions as well as witnessing an interesting demonstration of bird ringing. It was through the Society that I became interested in birds. I had always enjoyed watching them, but apart from a few very common Australian birds such as the magpie, galah, kookaburra, cockatoo and blue wren I had not known many birds by name, and even less about them. However, as I mentioned previously, we had so many beautiful birds at Crown Bird Creek I decided that we had to learn more about their habits. Here the society was a great help and Vic Smith provided us with a good deal of information. He worked as a veterinary scientist at Vom and later came to work in Australia. On his retirement he went to live near Albany in Western Australia, and only a year or so ago published a small book, *Portrait Of A Peninsula*, an account of the history and wild life of Torndirrup National Park, a small national park situated south of Albany. We still visit each other whenever possible.

Another interesting excursion organized by the Field Society was to see some rock paintings in the Bauchi Province. I had seen rock paintings in Australia and other parts of the world and they all seemed to have a certain similarity. They were generally drawings and paintings of animals that existed in the area at that time. For this reason I did not expect the Geje Paintings to be much different. I never discovered who actually found the paintings, but it was mainly through the work of the people working at Jos museum that an effort was made to ensure their preservation and protect them from vandals.

Very little was known about these paintings and most of the local people did not even know where they were. Whether the paintings had been done by a tribe living in the area at the time or whether itinerant people herding their cattle through the area had taken shelter under the overhanging cliff and painted the animals they were familiar with on the smooth rock face was not known. Although the paintings were rather indistinct, the cliff had sheltered them from the wind and rain and one could make out the shapes of the various animals depicted. There were monkeys, a cow and a horse and something that looked vaguely like an antelope or possibly a goat. They were painted with red and brown pigments, probably derived from the surrounding fields.

Although the paintings were interesting I was much more interested in a pagan village we passed by *en route* to the paintings. I had noticed some pagan women working on their farms a short distance away. They had very prominent features and appeared to be wearing helmets. They looked quite different from any pagan people I had seen previously. When we were returning and walking through the village the mystery was solved. This pagan tribe was notable for its women known as the 'duck-billed women'.

According to local stories in earlier times the women of the tribe had been noted for their handsome appearance; this made them a target for the slave traders, so to make them look less attractive a ghastly operation of mutilation had been practised. The lips of young girls were slit and wooden plugs were inserted. These plugs were never removed except when a larger plug was placed in position. They even ate with the plugs still in place. Some had similar plugs in their ears. It may have been a deterrent to the slavers but it was a hideous disfigurement and some of the girls lost their lives through blood poisoning when the operation was performed.

The peculiar helmet shaped heads had been achieved by something which could best be described as a permanent hair set. In this area there was a high quality clay which made excellent pots. The women of the tribe made these pots and they were sold in the local markets and provided a good source of revenue for the tribe. The clay was evidently regarded as also having some cosmetic value as they also used it to plaster down their hair and the resulting set was extremely durable.

Many other interesting lectures were given at the Field society's meetings, notably those by Bernard Fagg, Dr Gerry Dunger and Michael Cardew.

Two of the most interesting functions held on the Plateau were exhibitions by the well known French artist, Maurice Fievet. He was first an art master and later Professor of Fine Arts in Paris. He spent a number of years travelling all over Africa painting the people, animals, and scenery in the various countries. After his first expedition he won in 1950 the *Prix Louis Liotard* from the French Explorers Society, also the very high award for painting, the *Grand Prix des Beaux Arts*.

At the Imperial Institute in London the British government held an exhibition of three hundred of his paintings in oil. As a result of this exhibition he was asked to design a set of stamps for Nigeria. This set of twelve pictorial stamps was awarded the Silver Cup at the International

Philatelic Competition. Apart from his paintings, many of which have been used to illustrate books and features in prestigious magazines, M. Fievet also designed posters for various national parks in Africa and was also well known as a lecturer.

He painted many aspects of life in Northern Nigeria. The first exhibition was held not long after we went to live at Shen. Tony purchased one of his paintings, a portrait of a Hausa man, and gave it to me as a present. Some years later at a second exhibition a generous friend presented me with another of his paintings, a delightful study of a young Kanuri girl. Both pictures now adorn the walls of our lounge in Queensland.

The great social events for the Muslim population were the Sallas. The one held at the end of the month long fast of Ramadan was always an exciting event. Momo donned his best riga and his wife and daughters always had new clothes. One Salla almost ended in disaster for all their new finery. We had been spending a few days in Kaduna and on our return journey had a very bad trip back to Bukuru. The car, an old Pontiac, had given trouble for the entire journey. As we got near Bukuru we noticed that there had been a severe storm and by the time we reached the house at Zawan there was water everywhere. Both our house and Momo's were old buildings and far from waterproof. Every time it rained the roofs leaked like sieves and we had to get buckets and dishes to collect the water. When the storm burst Momo had tried to save our lounge carpet and protect the bed linen, but his wife Dada had been unable to prevent their Salla day finery from getting wet. The girls were upset and near to tears. Although I was tired after our awful trip from Kaduna something had to be done so Momo and I spent a good deal of the night ironing and airing clothes to get them dry. Anyway it was worth the effort as in the morning all went off happily to celebrate their big day.

A good deal of the social life, African and European, centred around the clubs provided by the company. The Yelwa Club at Bukuru had a snooker table, a bar, a dining-room and a library, and also provided meals and accommodation for visitors and people in transit, going on or returning from leave. The dining room when cleared provided ample space for dancing and the Scottish community held highland dances and dancing classes there. Sometimes exhibitions were held there, generally photography and painting, and on one occasion we had an exhibition of imported jewellery.

Sunday was usually the big day at the club. Most of the community went there for a social drink and a curry lunch. Curry lunches, either at the various clubs or in private homes, were very popular Sunday functions, but as Tony and I had grown very used to bush life we often varied the routine by taking a bush picnic. It gave Momo and Suli a break. We set off early and went to the various beauty spots around the Plateau. One popular spot was Assob Falls. Apart from being an attractive spot for a picnic one could, if one so wished, take a swim there. Because of the incidence of river blindness, the company had warned company personnel of the danger of swimming there. It was regarded as safe if one kept oneself covered after leaving the water, but it was not a risk either of us was prepared to take. Another risk was the prevalence of crocodiles in that area. A spot we often visited was Jekko. It was a hydro-electric generating station and it was at a lower elevation than where we lived on the Plateau and was considerably hotter, but the scenery was ruggedly interesting. Sometimes we went down to the little escarpment at the edge of the Plateau. It was rather a hair raising drive, but there were many beautiful trees and very lush tropical vegetation including many flowering trees and a variety of orchids.

Nearly everyone on the mine took part in some form of sport particularly at the weekends. The company had made provision for various sporting activities. Rugby and squash were very popular, and there were golf courses at Rayfield, Jos and Barakin Ladi. At one stage the company even had a sailing club using the local tin dams for this sport. Tennis courts had been built at both the company clubs and others were available in Jos. Bitumen cricket pitches had been laid down in various places and these were sometimes used for inter district matches. Activities at the Plateau Turf Club were also very popular and well patronized. Many of the Africans loved gambling, so the Turf Club was very popular. Polo was played on a limited scale, but the expense and the skill required put this beyond the reach of many.

The swimming pools at both clubs provided sport and recreation for both children and adults. As I was not a sport addict I took my exercise toiling in the garden. At one time we had a visit from two American ladies. They were very intrigued with one flower bed in our garden. It was a small bed edged with amethyst. Whenever I mention this amethyst bordered flower bed people often look amazed, but are too polite to say that they do not believe me. Many of the boulders found in the Rayfield area had encrustations of quartz crystals. This quartz when it contained minute quantities of manganese attained a beautiful shade of purple, amethyst, and made a most spectacular edging for a flower bed.

The ladies were so overcome when they saw the amethyst that they requested one of the boulders for a souvenir. I thought it was rather a weighty souvenir, but was more amazed when they casually mentioned that they were collecting rocks from around the world to make into a fireplace when they returned to the United States. I wondered how they transported these rocks, for if they went by air as excess baggage it was going to be one of the world's most expensive fireplaces. I suppose we all have a tendency to collect strange items. I collected china cats and my sister said that for anyone who moved about the world as much as we did it was a very odd hobby. However, apart from one or two minor accidents my china cats are still with me. Many were given to me by Nigerian friends and they bring back very happy memories.

Chapter 19

Education and Other Problems

One great problem for expatriates in Nigeria was the education of their children. In the early days of the mining operations there was of course no problem as there were few white women on the mines fields and virtually no children. After the Second World War there was a big influx of women and children. Improved medical facilities and more effective malarial prophylactics made the danger from malaria much less while yellow fever and smallpox were practically eliminated. With reasonable care young children could be kept quite healthy and there were adequate centres for education. The mining company had schools for African and European children while Marie Prescott, an excellent teacher, had a school for young children whose parents were not employed by A.T.M.N. This school which was known as Prescott's Academy did a splendid job with young pupils. In Jos there was a school managed by American missionaries. The school had a good reputation, but as most of the pupils were preparing to return to the United States the school curriculum was very much oriented to American education.

However, when the children reached the age of eleven they had to leave Nigeria to attend boarding schools, generally in England or other European countries, to obtain their secondary education. This separation from their parents placed a great strain on both parents and children, but fortunately when air travel became more commonplace many of the children returned to Nigeria for the longer school holidays thus making the separations less traumatic.

The African community, particularly the Ibos, Yorubas and some of the pagans were very keen on having their children educated as they knew that this was the only way they were going to occupy the higher paid positions in the government and the private companies, so most of

Momo, Wife and daughters in Sallah Day finery.

the children, boys and girls attended either government or mission schools.

I tried to get Momo interested in education for his daughters, and more importantly for his grand children. He was prepared to acknowledge that it might have some merit for boys, but thought it was quite unnecessary for girls. I pointed out to him that often, though his girls married young, education was always an asset. I told him that one of the girls who held down a good position at one of the larger stores had come down from the pagan village of the duck-billed women. Fortunately her father, obviously an intelligent man years ahead of his time, first of all would not allow the operation which had produced mutilation and death among the women of the tribe, but he also insisted that his daughter attend school. As a result the girl got a good position and also made a good marriage. I am afraid that I did not convince Momo on the value of education for girls.

Apart from education there were other day to day problems that had to be coped with. One morning Momo came in looking very worried and said his small grand daughter had found some pills and had eaten a lot of them. The only pills his grand daughter could have found were vitamin pills or some anti-malaria pills. Although neither were lethal in prescribed doses a quantity of them could have a serious effect on a small child. Anyway we wrapped the little girl in a blanket and with the two offending bottles of tablets set off for Jos. Dr Branch treated her and she soon recovered.

The problem with Ishiako was of a very different nature. Ishiako was our steward before Suli came to us. As a steward Ishiako was pretty hopeless, but he was a handsome, likeable young man so we put up with his shortcomings. One morning he failed to come in to help with breakfast and Momo said he was very ill. He certainly looked ill and Tony took him up to the mission hospital at Zawan. We had no idea what was wrong with him but finally we heard the full story. Ishiako was extremely worried that he had no children, and thought that it was a grave slur on his masculinity. Somewhere in the African market he had managed to buy a bottle of pills labelled 'Long Life and Power Pills'. The recommended dose was two pills daily, but Ishiako thought that there was nothing that two pills would do that a full bottle of pills would not do better, so he promptly swallowed the full bottle of pills. We could not find out much about this episode but Momo finally got the full story from Ishiako. Anyway, nature took its course and he recovered without hospital treatment, I never did find out whether or not the long life and power pills had the desired result as Ishiako left us about this time and was replaced by Suli. As a result the household ran much more smoothly.

Our next big upset was the loss of our beautiful Siamese cat, Warri Bhoko. It had been a long hot summer and the rains were late. I had noticed that the pagans seemed to be spending a great deal of time out hunting in the fields evidently looking for lizards and other small animals. Just outside our compound was a large outcrop of granite boulders and Warri used often to go out and sun himself on the rocks. He often slept there and I took little notice of his absence in the afternoon, but when he did not return for his evening meal I feared the worst.

Momo was quite sure the pagans had killed him as he said he had often seen them hunting for snakes and lizards around the rocks. I was, of course, very upset as Warri was probably the most beautiful cat we had ever owned and was loved by all who knew him. However, I had to look at it in a more practical light. The pagans were definitely meat hungry and a large sleeping cat was easy prey and I dare say that under similar circum-stances I might have been tempted to do the same myself. We were a long time getting over the loss of Warri, but fortunately because of people retiring, and not being able to take their animals into other countries, pets were passed on and eventually we acquired two more Siamese cats, Sooty and Tailu. These two gave us a lot of pleasure and remained with us until I left Nigeria. I had made arrangements for them to be passed on to other owners after Tony left the country but sadly both cats died. Tailu died of cancer, but we never did find out what happened to Sooty.

I mentioned that with the arrival of Suli our household ran very smoothly and happily. Momo and Suli and their respective wives and families agreed very well and the happy-go-lucky garden boy George was a friend to everyone. I thought it was too good to last and it was – Momo decided to take a second wife. I knew that the law and his religion did not forbid this, but I did not think that it was going to lead to domestic harmony. The new wife was a very young girl, younger than two of Momo's daughters and looked more like his grand child than his wife. It was not long before I noticed that the poor child was doing most of the work about the house. Dada, the senior wife gave up the monotonous task of grinding corn to make the African porridge, and the young wife seemed to be the one looking after the grand children. It was not long before she left. Later when I asked Momo where she had gone, he just said, 'I sack her.' Tony's headman, Mallam Hassan, probably had a better explanation when he said, 'The wife be too young and Momo be too old.'

Momo bore his loss with great fortitude, and never lost his sense of humour. Later I mentioned to him that he had a nice wife and family and asked him if he really needed another wife. He just replied, 'The law allows it and God does not forbid it.' I told him that I was prepared to accept that but asked him if he could afford to keep two wives. 'Not really,' he said, and then with a humorous glint in his eye he added, 'but with an increase in wages it would be possible.' After that remark we decided that further discussion of his matrimonial affairs was pointless.

Chapter 20

Tribal Massacres

Ever since the assassination of the Sardauna of Sokoto and the murder of the Prime Minister, Sir Abubakar Tafawa Balewa, there had been rumours of trouble between the Ibos and the Hausas. There was a considerable amount of tension in the air, and in the various larger towns and cities several ugly incidents had been reported.

Another rather disturbing feature was the number of people who seemed to be leaving the plateau. For some weeks I had watched the trains passing our home, and each day they seemed to be more and more crowded, people hanging on to the windows of the train, while the doors were blocked, and the roof was covered with passengers and their luggage. When I asked Momo why there were so many people on the trains he just said they were Ibos returning to their own country, the eastern region of Nigeria.

However, nothing prepared me for what was to happen one bright sunny morning. Tony had just left for work and I was talking to Momo, when his daughter, Dada Karima burst into the kitchen. This was more than unusual as Dada was a very polite girl, and always knocked at the door and waited for her father to invite her in. However, the poor girl was shaking, and just gasped out, 'There's war in Bukuru!' As Bukuru mining headquarters were only a mile or so down the road from our house, to say the least I received something of a shock, and this was something of an understatement. At that moment Tony arrived at the front door looking very upset and said Dada's news was quite true, that during the night a tribal massacre had started and Hausas were murdering Ibos. He had been driving to Bukuru when he had seen a freshly killed body by the side of the road. One of the Africans told him that there was murder and fighting going on around the railway station and in Bukuru township, so he decided to return to Rayfield Headquarters for instructions. The General Manager asked him to visit all European households to tell the women that the massacre had started and that bands of Africans were likely to visit each house looking for Ibos. If these mobs did arrive they were asked to allow two representatives to enter the house to make sure there were no Ibos hiding on the premises.

We always employed Hausa staff, but people who employed Ibo servants were placed in a truly dreadful situation. Tony arrived at one house just in time to see the Ibo steward killed by an angry mob. Momo's first reaction was that he wanted to go to Bukuru, evidently to see what was going on. I said a firm 'No' and told him that he was first to lock his wife and daughters in his house and then return to our kitchen as he was to have the job of escorting the African representatives around the house and garden while Suli and I made sure that they departed. Some time later I went into the garden and almost ran into two or three men, chasing a luckless Ibo who was caught and killed before my eyes as he was trying to escape.

I went inside, and feeling rather sick, hardly knew what to do, but decided that the best thing was to get as much water as possible boiled, filtered and stored in case of the failure of our electrical supply and the danger of contamination of our water supply. This chore kept Momo, Suli and me busy for most of the day.

Tony arrived home in the evening after a truly gruelling day, reassuring the wives of company employees that there would be no trouble as long as there were no Ibos on the premises and that they allowed the two representatives free access in their search. To their credit virtually all the wives kept their calm and obeyed company instructions. After visiting all the wives he then went down to the laboratory in Bukuru. As Bukuru along with Jos had borne the brunt of the massacre many of the staff were very much on edge and normal work was out of the question. Tony closed the laboratory until further notice and warned company employees to keep to their homes and out of trouble.

Because of the danger from infection and particularly pollution of water supplies from dead bodies he then had the unenviable task of checking as far as possible the number of dead, and with other members of company staff arranging for burial.

Two of our loyal staff from our days in bush, Momo Beri-Beri and Usman Dikwa were a big help to Tony in this gruesome task. Both Momo and Usman had been soldiers with the West African Regiment in the Burma campaign and were familiar with the horrors of war but although both were Hausas and Muslims they were deeply affected. Usman Dikwa was a man to whom the word 'gentleman' could be applied in the very best sense of the word. Like all Hausas while acknowledging that the Ibos had brought a great deal of the trouble on themselves he was truly appalled at the senseless slaughter.

An odd sideline to all this trouble was the curious behaviour of our animals. I had heard that during the Second World War in Britain animals seemed to have a knowledge of an approaching raid before the bombs were actually dropped. Our cats were extremely agitated just prior to, and during the massacre, their behaviour being at times quite frenetic.

People with Ibos in their employ had suffered horrific experiences. Among those who had suffered very badly were Marie and Bernard Prescott. Marie, who along with her husband had made us the beautiful cake for Roy Noel's twenty-first birthday so many years before, had established a school, Prescott's Academy for young children living on the Plateau. Bernard had become acting manager of the Nigerian Electric Supply Company (N.E.S.C.O.) As Marie employed Ibo servants in her house and school she had the dreadful experience of witnessing the massacre of her faithful retainers, while at the same time trying to shield her young charges from the horrifying sight.

Bernard had the vital job of keeping power going for the entire minefield and Plateau area. Because of his drastically reduced staff, most of whom had been Ibos, he had practically no sleep for several days. The young children did not suffer as much as we had expected. Indeed some of them reacted as if they were witnessing a real life Cowboys and Indians scene.

This particular massacre had lasted only for forty-eight hours but it left a marked impression on all those who had lived through it and we could never pretend that life on the mines field was ever the same again.

Gabriel told us that he had been terrified at the time. He was not an Ibo but a Yoruba. However, he looked rather like an Ibo, and he decided that the safest thing he and his wife could do was lock themselves inside their house and stay there. It was a wise decision. After the massacre he stayed on working for A.T.M.N. for some time but he told us that he was contemplating a move back to his own country. Shortly after we returned to Australia Gabriel wrote to say that he was going back to Oyo. He is still living there.

As Ibos had made up most of the junior clerical staff, A.T.M.N., their places could not be filled immediately and the General Manager, asked Mary Thorogood and me to go to the office to count money and pay out the African workers. It was rather an eerie experience as Bukuru, a town usually seething with activity, seemed in a state of shock. Very few people were around and it was unnaturally quiet. It was hard to realize that two days before it had been the scene of a bloody massacre. The railway station where so many people and been killed was practically deserted.

The after effects told on people in many different ways. A dear friend of mine whose Ibo servant died in her arms took a mild stroke, while others, including Tony, lost a considerable amount of weight, some put on weight and others came out in rashes. We nearly all smoked more heavily. For the first time since my arrival in Nigeria I found myself growing irritable with Momo, Suli and some of my European friends. However, they all bore it well and after a European holiday I felt much better.

A friend in Jos told me that one group of people who really must have wondered what was happening was a number of Italians. At that time the railway line was being extended through Jos to the far northern town of Maiduguri, and the contract had been let out to various firms, and among the workers on the section through Jos were these Italians. On the first day of the massacre some of them had come into Jos to collect their stores and found themselves in the middle of a 'Civil War'. As none of them could speak either English or Hausa they had simply no idea of what was going on. I was later told that after considerable pandemonium and much excited shouting stores were forgotten about and the group made a hurried exit back to their camp.

After the massacres in Bukuru and Jos there were sporadic outbursts of trouble in various parts of Northern Nigeria. One young man who was arriving from England to work for A.T.M.N. had brought with him a book to read on the plane. It was entitled *How to Keep a Stiff Upper Lip.* He probably needed the advice for when the plane landed at Kano, his first experience at the airport was having two Africans murdered and dying at his feet. Another group of people returning from leave were greeted by a soldier who boarded the plane saying, 'All Europeans leave the plane.' One lass told me that she thought that they were all going to be shot on the spot, but later heard that they were clearing the plane of all the passengers except Ibos. During and after the massacre there was a good deal of the looting of the homes of Ibos who had occupied various positions in firms in Jos, as well as those working for mining companies, the smelter and some agencies on the Plateau. In some cases the houses were virtually demolished, windows smashed, doors torn off and anything moveable removed.

We decided after witnessing some of this looting in Bukuru that we would send some of our effects back to England. Our friends Mary and John Pulling had left Nigeria just prior to the massacres and had purchased a home in England. They were glad of a few extra pieces of furniture. The precious Fievet paintings were removed from their frames, rolled and later reframed in England.

When things were comparatively calm again we had a long discussion with Momo as to why such a dreadful series of events could ever have happened. He said that the Ibos had come up to the Plateau and had taken all the best jobs. I tried to point out that they had probably got the jobs because they were keener on education than the predominantly Muslim Hausas and were therefore better qualified to take the positions, but Momo did not see it that way at all. The fact that Hausa people could not do the jobs did not seem to Momo to have any bearing on the case. He just said that the Hausa people should have the jobs in their own country. Of course at the back of his mind was the killing of the Sardauna of Sokoto, the spiritual leader of the Muslims and the torture and murder of the highly revered Sir Tafawa Balewa. These crimes were never forgiven by the Hausas.

After the massacre there was an increase in the military presence in various towns and cities and several ugly incidents were reported in the local press. One night we had a rather unpleasant experience. We had been out to dinner at a friend's place near Barakin Ladi and on the way home were stopped by an armed soldier who asked if we could give him a lift back to Bukuru. He carried an army rifle, and as he was sitting at my back with the weapon only a few inches from my head I fervently hoped that his hand would not shake. When we reached Bukuru he wished us a cheery 'Good Night' and got out of the car still firmly grasping his rifle. We were not sorry to see him go.

Another aspect of life which was more a nuisance than anything else was being constantly stopped by the military at road blocks to have the car searched. It was bearable during the dry season, but once the rains started, climbing in and out of the car in the middle of a deluge was not so funny, but as the soldiers were armed it was not advisable to argue with them.

When I was travelling on a bus to Kano airport the military decided to search the entire bus and the passengers. We were told to open all bags, cases, etc. Seated next to me was a German missionary who did not have the faintest idea what the soldier was saying, and as none of his fellow passengers could speak German I think the poor man thought his end had arrived when he was rather roughly handled, his suitcase snatched from him and its contents searched. Years later I was reminded of this when we underwent a similar military type search. We were crossing the frontier from Bulgaria to Turkey. Many people from Bulgaria were trying to escape to other countries. A burly armed military gentleman got on the bus, forcibly hustled the passengers off and stamped up and down the central aisle of the bus. They evidently suspected that people were hidden under the floor.

As he was a big, heavy man I rather hoped that with all the stamping he would fall through the floor of the bus. The Nigerian search was almost a pleasure compared with this one.

After the massacre some people retired prematurely and others left to take up positions in other countries but we decided to stay on until Tony's retirement.

Chapter 21

Leaving Nigeria

With the approach of Tony's fifty-fifth birthday we knew that our long stay in Nigeria would soon be over as 55 was the normal retiring age for expatriates working in Nigeria. As his birthday occurred in the middle of his tour, he would probably have remained a little longer, but he received a call from London office to report as soon as convenient to London. When we arrived there, the directors offered Tony the job of setting up an exploration Department in Australia for the parent company, London Tin Corporation. The office in Australia was a subsidiary of London Tin called A.O. Australia. Its main function was to act as a buying agency and a liaison office for A.O. Malaya and A.O.N. Nigeria, but as there was a mining boom in Australia at the time they were anxious to expand their operations in Australia. Tony had to return to Nigeria to finalize his affairs and prepare his department for his successor. I left a few months before Tony as I was returning to Australia by sea, and most of our heavy baggage including the items sent to England after the tribal massacres had to be collected and packed ready for shipment. The faithful Momo was paid off and received the financial bonus we had been saving for him over the years.

I felt very sad when the time came to leave as the eighteen happiest years of my life had been spent in Nigeria and I had formed many close and lasting friendships. When I went to say goodbye to Momo, Suli and their families I don't think they fully realized that I would not be returning, but thought that I was going on leave again and would be back in a few months.

I flew to London and after a few weeks of hectic farewells, packing up etc. I had to make a train journey to Liverpool where I boarded the *Port Brisbane* and prepared for the long voyage back to Australia, by way of

Cape Town, Port Elizabeth, Durban and Lourenco Marques. It was a happy trip. There were only seven passengers on board and we spent a few days in each port as the vessel was predominantly a cargo ship and loading and unloading took up a considerable amount of time in each port. My last view of Africa came as we sailed out of Lourenco Marques. I stood on the deck of the ship until the African coastline receded from sight. I was leaving a large part of my life behind.

*   *   *

Since our return to Australia we have travelled extensively in Europe, Asia and the Pacific region including an unforgettable trip on the Trans-Siberian railway from Kharbarovsk to Moscow. I have never returned to Africa apart from brief stopovers in Nairobi and Dar-es-Salaam airports when we were travelling to the Seychelles. I prefer to keep my memories.

Tony has made a visit to South Africa partly out of desperation. He had never previously visited the country and he grew rather tired of people asking him about the political conditions in South Africa. They always looked rather amazed when he told them that he had never been there and so could not comment. It was rather difficult for them to realize that Jos was closer by air to the European cities of Rome and Barcelona than to the South African cities of Johannesburg and Capetown.

After setting up the department for A.O. Australia Tony did exploration work all over Australia, first with A.O. Australia and later with Sampey Exploration and finally as a freelance consultant on alluvial mining. When the mining boom collapsed he returned to teaching with Ipswich Grammar and the Queensland Education Department. When retirement came the second time around he still worked as a consultant in alluvial mining.

Just about the time that I thought my pioneering days were over Tony took a job as a mining geologist at Noble's Nob, a remote gold and copper mine some miles from Tennant Creek in the Northern Territory of Australia. As the original contract was for only six weeks Tony decided that it would be best for him to go on his own while I looked after our Brisbane home.

However, at the end of six weeks I received a letter saying that Tony had agreed to stay on for three months. Tony wrote that he thought it would be better if I came out to Noble's Nob. Cooking was never Tony's forte and I gathered that he was getting pretty fed up with the meals supplied at the mine's dining room. I think I must have spoilt him with the meals I prepared for him. Fortunately his sister, living in Brisbane at the time was delighted to come into our house and look after the house, our two cats and the garden. This solved the problem on the Brisbane front but arrangements had to be made to get me to Noble's Nob. I asked the mining company to send me on the shortest possible route. When the airline told me that I would be travelling via Townsville, Cairns, Mt. Isa and Alice Springs and on to Tennant Creek I thought that if that was the shortest route I would hate to think of the longest.

Armed with a considerable amount of baggage I eventually reached Tennant Greek and from there the journey to Noble's Nob was completed by car. Once again I had to admit that at first sight the house provided was something of a shock. It was certainly not a mud or grass hut such as we had sometimes had in Africa but was something known as a de-mountable. As it was painted black it gave me the impression of a concentration camp hut. However, I have to admit that the inside was a pleasant surprise. It was fully air-conditioned, an unheard of luxury in Mt. Isa and Nigerian days. Furniture in the bedrooms, kitchen and bathroom was adequate and the lounge, although basic was moderately comfortable. An added bonus was an inside laundry.

The garden consisted of what appeared to be two small dead trees and a starved looking eucalyptus. The clothes line was sited in such a position that given a high wind I had the feeling that I would take off and be blown non-stop to Darwin some thousand miles to the north of us. However, having lived in much worse conditions I thought that I would survive quite nicely for the remainder of Tony's three month contract. Once again I received my usual surprise. The three months had been extended to six.

As soon as I heard that we would be at Nobles Nob for six months I decided that first of all something would have to be done about getting some greenery around the house and secondly we would have to get a cat. Tony soon found a cat. It was a delightful animal, and as a young cat had been very well looked after, having been neutered, given immunization shots and lots of tender, loving care. The owners later decided to return to England and passed the cat, then known as Pushkin, on to some people living on the mine site. They promised to give the cat a good home, but unfortunately the promise was not kept and Pushkin was only rescued in the nick of time as he was about to be 'put down'. Not only did he get a good home but he also got a change of name as we renamed him Terra.

Getting something growing was not so easy. Short of using explosive or a rock drill there was little I could do with the rock hard ground so I decided to concentrate on the nearly dead trees. I was pleasantly surprised, for after soaking them with all our waste water, the trees eventually began to sprout green leaves. I then discovered that they were flame trees (Poinciana) and their fernlike foliage greatly improved the appearance of the front of our house. Unfortunately I did not see them in flower as we left the mine before the flowering period in December and January.

On my first shopping trip to Tennant Creek I purchased a hanging basket and a few pot plants. Kind friends gave me a few more and the back porch soon became a small conservatory.

As the mine had originally been an underground mine, but was then opencast a considerable amount of blasting had to be done to remove the overburden. This exercise was usually performed once a week. An hour prior to the explosion a warning like an air raid siren was sounded.

This was a signal to turn off electrical appliances, grab washing off the line and board any vehicle to travel to the far end of the mine to a safe site. As most of the houses were built very close to the mining excavation it was far too dangerous to remain in them as large boulders were sometimes flung into the air by the blasting and many buildings bore scars showing where rocks had gone through them. Some people took their pets with them to the safer areas, but Terra did not have to be taken for as soon as the siren sounded he dived under the house and remained there until I returned after the 'all clear' was sounded. Because of the heavy pall of red dust from the explosion it was necessary that all washing be taken inside. There was never a regular schedule for the blasting and it could be any day of the week and any time of the day.

Life at the mine was very quiet but as there was an excellent library at Tennant Creek I was able to catch up on my reading. As we had the feeling that our six months stay at the mine could easily turn into twelve months Tony insisted that he was to return to Brisbane not later than the end of October as neither of us wanted to spend the long sweltering summer in Central Australia.

When the time came to leave, our biggest problem was Terra. We could not find a suitable home for him so it was decided that he would return to Brisbane with us. I left a few days before Tony and took most of the luggage with me while he travelled with Terra on the Lear jet at a later date. I gathered that the journey was rather traumatic for both of them. It was a long journey via Alice Springs, Adelaide, Sydney and Brisbane and Terra did not take kindly to flying. He raised a commotion when interviewed by Tony at every airport and when the crowning indignity came at Brisbane and he was placed on the roundabout with all the airline baggage his howls could be heard all around the baggage room.

However he settled down well to his new home and although he is now thirteen years old he is still with us. He is a bright and happy cat well known to all our friends and very popular in the neighbourhood.

Noble's Nob was my last pioneering experience. Tony did his final geological job in New Zealand and then retired. Like most women I have never retired. I still maintain a house and garden plus the inevitable cats.

In the garden we have planted several of the trees and flowers we grew in Nigeria. In most tropical gardens the trees and flowers grown are the same the world over, and the jacaranda, frangipanni, bauhinnias and many others still remind me of my very much loved home at Crown Bird Creek.

A pleasant feature of our life in Brisbane is that over the years we have been able to entertain a number of our friends from our Nigerian days. Some have settled in various parts of Australia and some have visited us from overseas.

Three years ago we received a very pleasant surprise when Revd. Walter Erbeles' son and daughter-in-law came to see us. We had last seen Terry Erbele when he was a student at Hill Crest school in Jos. He and his wife now live in Oregon in the United States of America.

I still try to keep in touch at least once a year with all my old friends. Although they are now scattered world-wide their letters and cards bring back memories of the happy times we shared together and also provided most of the happenings recorded in this story.

I thank you all.